# I LET MY SOUL RUN FREE!

# MY JOURNEY TO BECOMING

# WHOLE

# I LET MY SOUL RUN FREE

ISBN:978-0-359-10422-2

# CONTENTS

# 1

## I SHED MY LAST TEAR!

*No more crying because time has already passed me by.*

*No more anxiety about how fast time seems to fly*

*No more pleading to God to answer my questions why because I know He sees the pain and the tears that I cry.*

*No longer will I be controlled by fear, because now it is my Lord and Savior that I hold to me so dear. This is it; I have shed my last tear.*

*No more will I mourn the years that have passed away; no more will I stumble in the dark, because I now know the way.*

*No more worries about how long someone chooses to stay I am now on my own*

*journey so its okay if you need to walk away.*

*This is it for me; I now understand why I am here so don't you worry about me, because I have shed my last tear.*

# I LET MY SOUL RUN FREE

Sitting in this beautiful church, watching several of my classmates walk across the stage to get their diplomas, I begin to ponder my future and wonder what it will feel like when I walk across this stage to receive my degree in Theology. It was a year ago when I started classes here, and now with one year under my belt, I am ready to start year number two. I love the professors and the classes that I have taken and I am excited about where this is going to lead me.

Eighteen months before visiting Beulah, I was so fed up with my job that on several occasions I was tempted to just leave my badge with the secretary, walk out and never return. I had a stirring deep down inside and I couldn't figure out what it was, but it was something that I couldn't ignore. On some level I knew that it was more than my job that had me feeling this way, but I didn't know what it was. I knew that I felt like there was more to my life than my current career.

Don't get me wrong, I love being a paramedic! I was twelve, the first time I can recall seeing an ambulance ride by. I could see a man in the back, working on a patient, and at that moment I said, "That is what I want to do when I grow up." After working a few places, I finally went to school to become a paramedic and I have worked in this field for over twenty-seven years. Now I find myself walking the halls of the emergency room, wondering is there more to life, more importantly, is there more to me, than this?

Over the years I have seen talk shows where they featured guests that had very successful, careers that paid well; then one day they decided to leave and do something different and it turned out to be the best decision they had ever made.

They dared to go against the norm of having a steady job for forty years that they could retire from, to saying the heck with that, I am going to do something I always wanted to do. Against the advice of family and friends, they did just that, and now they are living their dream.

So- I decided I was going to leave my job and I began preparing myself for my departure. The first thing I did was leave the house I was living in and move in with my best friends. I was in a good place in my life. I didn't have much debt, just the car that I had recently bought, nothing else. I was unsure where I wanted to work and where I was going to live, so I didn't want to be tied down with a lease. Friends and family thought that I had lost my mind and to be honest with you, I thought I had lost my mind too. Here I am fifty-two years old and I am living with friends.

What people didn't understand was that I had been living on my own since I was nineteen, and I was tired of being alone. I wanted to have someone to talk to and to eat dinner with and just be social. Also, this was the first time in my life that I felt like I had the world at my feet instead of on my back.

I could do anything I wanted, and live anywhere I wanted. This was the first time that I could make a decision that wasn't based in fear, so I just wanted to sit back and breathe for a second while I decided where my life was going to go next. I sold all my furniture, packed up my things and put them in storage, and dropped off my dog, Sprit, to my best friend's niece's house.

The house was beautiful and spacious, and the company was great, but every day, while I lay in bed, I would ask myself, what are you doing? Why are you doing this? I never had an answer to these questions and I often wondered if my family and friends were right. Had I lost it? But I didn't change my

mind and I desperately needed to take my time and make a sound decision on what I was going to do next. I had been living there about a week, when those questions came up again. What are you doing? Why are you doing this? This time I realized that I needed some help in making a decision that was going to affect the next stage of my life.

Instead of asking my sister or asking friends, I got out of bed and got on my knees and began to pray. I started off with the Lord's Prayer, and then I did something that I had never done before. I began talking to God about my life. I told God about feeling empty. I told Him that I didn't have a plan for this next stage in my life. So I asked God, what His plan for my life is. I told Him that whatever it is, I promise I will do it. I finished up my prayers and got back into bed and went to sleep. An hour or so later, my cell phone rang. I didn't recognize the number, but answered it anyway. It was a Theology school that I contacted a couple of years earlier requesting information concerning their Theology program.

I looked up at the ceiling and said, "Really God? Theology!" I spent a few minutes asking the gentleman about their program and was a little disappointed when I found out that their school didn't have an undergraduate program. In the back of my mind I said, "Well, that's that. I tried and that didn't work out." How quickly I was ready to give up on God when I had asked Him for help. I went back to sleep and for the next couple of weeks I was still feeling troubled about my current situation.

A month or so later, I moved; and went to live with another great friend who lived about an hour north of where I was staying. I am sure I set the gossip line on fire with this move. I know they really thought I had lost my mind when I moved again and didn't get my own place. But the truth of the matter is… nothing had changed. I still wanted company and I still had no idea what I was going to do with my life.

While I was staying at the new place, those same two questions began to haunt me again. Every day I would lie in bed and ask myself, "What are you doing? Why are you doing this?"

Then one day, while I was lying in bed, trolling Facebook, I decided to Google some theology schools in the area- just to see what was out there. There were plenty of online programs, but I wanted to be in a classroom where I could interact with the students and the professors face-to-face.

Prior to this, I had no plans of ever going back to school. After I graduated with my Associates Degree, that was supposed to be it for me. I continued to surf the Web for about twenty minutes before deciding on a theological college downtown. I found the number and I called. The lady that answered the phone told me all about the course. She told me that the course lasts eight months and cost $200 for each segment. She informed me that the first segment starts up again in late August. It was May so I had some time to think about it. I thanked her for the information and let her know that I would see her soon.

I continued to work while I waited for my class to start. I noticed that I wasn't feeling as frustrated at work; perhaps because I was looking forward to this class. In preparation for the class, I began to study the Bible. I looked up unfamiliar words to get their meaning and I also began looking up words that I thought I knew the meanings of. I was shocked at how the definitions differed from what I thought they meant, especially when applied to the scripture that I was studying. I noticed that I would get goose bumps when I read certain scriptures and I became excited when I understood the concepts that the scripture was teaching me.

August came around quickly and I drove downtown to the school for my first class. I was very excited! I had purchased my books and I had a notebook and new pens. The class was three hours long and we met once a week, during the evening. The class was large and filled with about twenty-five students, twenty of which were either pastors or they were getting ready to be ordained in the next couple of months. The other five students were lay people, like me.

As I sat in class, surrounded by all those pastors, I felt a little bit out of place. I had just started to read the Bible and I had not been to a church service in ten years. Even though I had no idea how all of this worked, I stayed and continued to attend class. We studied scripture and church history. I was learning a lot, but it wasn't until the last day of the eight-month course that I discovered why I was there.

We had been told since the first day of school that we would be writing a nine-minute sermon at the end of the eight months. I was very nervous about this, which was surprising because I love to write and between my poetry and motivational speaking I was used to speaking in public. However, this was very different for me because I was going to be speaking about the Word of God, which I was just beginning to learn.

During the last month of the program we began working on

our sermons. The instructor said we could pick any scripture in the New Testament. When writing our sermon, we have to have a setting, a situation, and a solution followed by a celebration then a conclusion-this is the common format. He also wanted us to use a personal story to help the listener understand how the scripture applied to our life. When he added the last statement about the personal story, I asked him if it had to be a personal story or could it be another story that really brings home the message of the scripture. He said he really wanted it to be a personal story.

Driving home from class that night, I was trying to figure out how I was going to write my sermon without using my story, but instead, use the story I had already planned to use. I had chosen to do my sermon on what Jesus said on the cross before He was crucified, "Forgive them Father for they know not what they do!" I already knew how I was going to write it; I just needed to do the celebration. On the morning of the day of my sermon, I got up, planning to quickly type the sermon that I was going to do in class that night. As I started to write the celebration portion, my plan suddenly changed.

In class that night, I gave the first part of my sermon- the setting, the situation and the solution- but for the celebration, I was simply honest and I told the class exactly how I came to write this part of my sermon. I started by saying that last week in class I was expressing my desire to talk about someone else to bring the message about how important forgiveness is, but professor Thomas was insisting that he wanted to hear how the scripture impacted me personally.

When I got home that night, I thought I had finagled a way to write this sermon the way I wanted to, and I believed I had it all figured out up until 10:55 this morning when I sat down to write my sermon and God stepped in and changed the story. You see I didn't want to tell my story because I had been delivered from it. I no longer suffered from the effects of the sexual abuse that I endured as a child. That was my cross to carry and I carried it for over forty-two years.

For forty-two years all I knew was darkness, depression and despair, now I am free of it, so I stored it away because it no longer pertained to me. So, this morning, when I opened my computer, this is what I wrote, "Do you think I allowed you to carry all of that pain for that amount of time for nothing?" Stephanie, it was never about you! I have a job for you to do and the job requires job experience.

When you tell your story, you need to tell them how much you suffered and that it took you forty-two years to

come through it.  Make sure you tell them, that during those forty-two
years, you tried everything but Me!  You need to tell them that the drugs and alcohol didn't work!  Tell them that the therapy and hypnosis didn't work!  Tell them that the new age religion, with its pyramids and crystals didn't work!

Tell them that it wasn't until you turned your life over to Me, forgave all parties involved and buried yourself in My Word, that I reached into the deepest parts of your heart, where all of that hurt, darkness, and despair was festering, and I removed it completely- leaving no residual evidence that it was ever there in the first place. You see, when you testify about what happened to you and how forgiving those who hurt you, took all of the hurt and pain away, you will lead those who are hurting, to Me!

Through you, I can heal those who have gone through the same ordeal or similar traumas!   Through you, they will see that there is not an offense so painful, so heinous or an offense buried so deep, that I can't reach in and heal it!  Through you they will know that what is said in the Bible is true!  When I stopped typing, I sat there looking amazed at what was on the screen, because this was not the story I was going to tell.

Then I gave my conclusion: Forgiveness is not a
skill that has to be practiced or developed and it is not a
gift- forgiveness IS a choice. You either choose to forgive
someone or you don't. Jesus didn't exclude certain
offenses; He said forgive them. So if you choose not to
forgive, then you have chosen to carry pain. When people
tell you that something is unforgivable, or that someone
doesn't deserve your forgiveness, think about where you
would be right now if God took that same attitude with you.

While writing that sermon, I knew that message was
for me, and I knew what my purpose was and why I had
such a long journey. I finished up by telling them that
forgiveness is the brightest light that you can shine on a
dark situation. After class, I asked Mr. Thomas if he could
recommend a theology school that had a Bachelors of Arts
program in Theology. When I got home that night, I
looked them up on my computer and sent away for an
admission packet. A few days later, I received the
application along with two reference forms to fill out. I
filled out all of the information and called to make an
appointment to tour the school. A few days later I was on
campus attending the chapel service.

After Chapel, the Director of Student Life took me
to her office to talk about attending Beulah Heights

University. The school is very small, which is perfect for me, because I like to have access to staff and faculty. When I was younger, I didn't do well at the larger universities. She started off by telling me a little more about Beulah Heights and how they started out as a Bible college ninety-eight years ago.

By the time we had finished talking, it was decided that I would be attending that summer, which was going to start in about forty-five days. I finished filling out admission forms, paid the required fees and walked over to the financial aid office. This was a new experience for me. My mother paid for my school in cash each semester when I went to college the first time. When I went for my associates, ten years later, I paid cash for my classes. School was a lot cheaper in those days, as I quickly found out.

The lady in the financial aid office was very nice and she told me how to access FAFSA and fill it out and assured me that she was there to help me in any way she could. She even offered to sit down and fill it out with me. I told her I would be fine. The friend I was living with was currently going to school online and could help me if I ran into any difficulties. She gave me some more information about how to find link to the financial aid website on the Beulah Heights website, and I left.

Four weeks later I was back on campus with all of my financial aid papers and assessment tests done. Now it was time to schedule orientation because school was going to start in two weeks. As I sat in the Student Life Directors office filling out more paper work, she asked me if I was going to be staying on campus.

I laughed and said, "No!" Then I asked jokingly, "You have dorms for old people?" She chuckled and replied, "The average age here is forty years old. Are you able to stay on campus?" I thought about my current living situation, and said, "Yes!"

We left the building and crossed the street and walked up the stairs of a beautiful six-bedroom house. It was really nice inside. It had two bedrooms on the first floor and four bedrooms on the second. She told me that everyone has their own room, with a desk and bookshelves. Two people share a bathroom. There are two refrigerators in the kitchen and there are three people to a fridge. The living room is furnished and has a computer and a flat screen television. There is also a furnished dining room, a basement, and a deck on the back.

I LET MY SOUL RUN FREE

These were definitely not the kind of dorms I was used to seeing. I told her that I wanted to stay on campus. She said that there was a waiting list, but because of how far I have to travel to get there, she would put me on the top of the list. We went back to the office and I put in my application for the dorm room and paid for the background check. As I walked back to my car I thought to myself, "So it begins!" As I drove home, the excitement was growing and I began looking forward to driving six minutes to work instead of ninety and I would just have to walk across the street to go to class.

I would have never guessed that I would be taking this route, especially at this time in my life. Not only will I be going back to school at the age of fifty-three, but I will be staying on campus as well. I knew that I was where God wanted me to be. I will let all those people continue to wonder why I am doing what I am doing and try to figure out how I came to this point in my life, because I already know exactly how I came to this.

# 2

## THE HUNTER

*Thirty-seven years ago I met a hunter, I did not know that's what he was at the time, you see this hunter was clever. He camouflaged himself as a friend, masked his scent with trust and blended into the surroundings unnoticed. This pleased him so he did it over and over again without any regard for the damage he was doing to me. This is how a hunter thinks, they live in the here and now, they do what makes them feel good no matter what the cost is to someone else. What's frightening is there are thousands of these hunters walking among us every day; they live in the darkness and they survive in our secrets. Somehow they know our weaknesses and our vulnerabilities and they use them to help trap us.*

*I have learned that there is a difference between these hunters and the hunters of animals. People who hunt animals are merciful. They don't let an animal suffer needlessly. They quickly put them out of their misery. Hunters of people just aren't as kind; they feed for a while, and then they stop, leaving your chest wide open. They stand over you and watch your soul bleed into the ground while you are lying there gasping for some understanding; then they walk away. They walk away knowing that you won't die but also knowing that every day that you live you, will wish you had. This is what it is like to be hunted; this is what it is like to be prey!*

# I LET MY SOUL RUN FREE

I was around seven when we moved to Gravestone. We were moving to our first house. My sister and brother protested the move at first, because they didn't want to leave their friends or their school. My mother had found a way for us to have our own home, so we wouldn't have to live in a house with two other families- thanks to her new job. My sister and brother finally agreed that this move is what was best for everyone, especially since things had become more dangerous at the house where we were living.

The new house was on McLaren Street. It was a three–bedroom, one-bath house with a one-car garage, a medium size yard, with a tree in the back that was made for climbing. On the back of the house, beneath one of the bedroom windows, was a set of storm doors that led down into the basement through the laundry room. The basement was dark and scary and had a long staircase that led upstairs. Next to the staircase was a door that led to the garage.

Life on McLaren Street was quiet and fun. There were several kids my age living on our block and I spent my days playing and running around the neighborhood with my two best friends- Steve and Todd. We played football, basketball, soccer and a game we made up called army. Over the next year or so, we saw families come and go and we always looked forward to meeting any new kids that were moving in.

Martin moved into the neighborhood about two years after we did. He lived with his uncle, a teenage cousin and a five-year-old niece. I remember the first time I saw him. He didn't look that much older than us because of his size, but actually he was older than my brother which made him about fifteen years old. He was short and slim, wore gold wire-rimmed glasses and he had a weird haircut. Martin didn't fit in with my brother and his friends because most of them were tall, broad and athletic, so he ended up hanging around us.

Unlike my friends, I was from a single-family home. My father died a little over a month before I turned one year old. When he died, my mom was left with three kids to rear on her own. My mother had to work long hours to keep food on the table and a roof over our heads. She attended school at night so that she could better herself and make more money so that she could give us the opportunities that she didn't have growing up.

My friends and I were all latch key kids, a term coined to refer to children who were left at home alone after school while their parents worked. I would come home after school and let myself in with the key that was pinned to the inside of my clothes. My daily routine, during the week, was to come home, change my clothes, eat something, do my homework, and before going outside, I was supposed to do my chores- which I rarely did.

What I didn't know was that my daily schedule was about to change drastically. You see, Martin took a real interest in me. He was always there when no one else was available to play with me. He would invite me to walk with him to the store and as a reward he would buy me candy or soda and sometimes he bought pizza. While we walked to the store, I would tell him everything that happened at school that day. He always seemed to be interested in what I was learning about.

Weeks later he would ask me about a test I was supposed to have in one of my classes, and when I told him my grade, he would say, "I knew you were smart." I thought it was kind of cool having someone older than me who wanted me around and I enjoyed the attention he gave me, and I really enjoyed that he didn't call me a tomboy. He enjoyed watching me play, and would tell me that I am a great athlete.

I wasn't like the other girls in the neighborhood, or in school for that matter- a fact that I was reminded of daily all because I played sports, the same sports that the guys played, and I was good. So I was put into a category of my own- a category that sometimes left me feeling alone and outside of the world. I did have a few female friends, but I spent most of my time with the guys because I loved to play basketball and football and soccer, but in the late 60's and early 70s, female athletes were not as readily accepted as they are today.

Contrary to popular belief, at least in my case, the guys I hung out with never forgot I was a girl. When we were playing football or basketball, I was expected to play like one of the guys, but I was never treated like one of the guys. In fact, when another guy on the court did or said something out of line, Todd was quick to put them in check. Plus playing sports with the guys helped me to become a better athlete.

When I played ball for the school, I loved hearing the crowd cheer when I put a move on an opponent leaving them in the dust while I broke to the basket for an easy layup or a pull up jump shot that was nothing but net. It was when I played sports that I felt special, but once the game was over, I would ride the late bus home alone- my brief moment of acceptance quickly dissipating as I watched the scenery whip by through the bus window.

Martin never treated me differently and I never felt that way when we hung out. He enjoyed watching me play so I always felt comfortable when I was around him. It was during these times that I felt it was okay to be me. So, for over a year he patiently waited for the groundwork to be set.

He now knew my schedule and the schedule of my family.

He had my trust and friendship

and the only thing left to do was for him to wait for an

opportunity to strike.

One warm summer day, I was outside playing by myself, neither Todd or Steve was home. Martin came out and we began playing a game that Martin made up, supposedly to test my eye hand coordination and my ball handling skills. I was very confident about athleticism and about my basketball skills and when challenged, I could talk trash with the best of them. So after a few rounds of who is going to beat whom, and how bad we were going to beat each other, we started the game.

We battled back and forth. He would win a game and I would win a game. It was a best of seven tournament and we were tied three games apiece. I started the seventh game off great. He was struggling to get by me and I was about to win, just one point away from victory and pizza, which was my reward for winning. If he wins, he gets a kiss on the cheek, his usual reward for the rare times he won. Suddenly, Martin became a new player and he scored five consecutive points and won the game easily.

I was very disappointed that I lost because I really wanted that pizza. He teased me a bit and then told me good game. He invited me to come inside and get something to drink. After gathering up my things, I had to run to catch up with Martin because he was already in front of his house. Martin lived just one house away from me in a two-story white house that he shared with a female cousin, a five-year-old niece, and an uncle. His uncle wore a hat and drove a station wagon, and that is all I remember about him because he was never home.

Along the right side of the house was a long gravel driveway that led to a broken down two-car garage that had a room connected to it that Martin called the playroom. When you went inside the front door of his house, there was a large wooden staircase to the left that led upstairs and to the right was the living room and down a short hall was the kitchen. We walked into the living room to a door that was just before the kitchen on the left that led down into the basement. I had been inside his house many times with Steve and Todd, but this was the first time I was by myself, but I didn't think anything of it.

I welcomed the break from the sun and looked forward to having something cold to drink, so I followed him down the stairs to get the soda. We descended the long wooden stairs into the dark basement. It smelled of old clothes and mold and I felt like I was suffocating. I asked him to turn on the light so that I could see where I was going. He said he was looking for the switch. Laughing I told him to stop playing and get the soda so that we could go back outside and I could avenge my loss.

But, he continued to play like he didn't know where the light switch was; then he disappeared into the darkness and I could no longer see him. I gave up begging for him to hurry and began to play along- pretending to help him find the switch. I stumbled through the dark basement with my hands sliding along the wall to balance me and hoping to find the switch before Martin did.

Martin was always thinking up little games to play and it was cooler down here than outside even though it was a little scary. I slowly made my way around the basement, trying to find him and the light switch. I ran into some boxes and hit my hip on a wooden table. A lightning bolt of pain shot down my leg. Now I wasn't having as much fun and I begged him to please turn on the light before I hurt myself again. In the far corner of the basement I ran into an old roll of carpet; I didn't know that Martin was waiting for me there until he grabbed me and started kissing me.

Wait! This was not the kiss on the cheek that I usually had to give him whenever he beat me, which again was rare. I fought for him to let go of me, but he fought just as hard to hold on. He wasn't saying anything just breathing real hard and fast and his hands were going places they shouldn't. I continued to fight but a nine-year-old girl is no match against a sixteen-year-old boy, but I didn't give up.

My mind was whirling as I tried to comprehend what was going on and I continued to struggle to get free. What kind of game is this? Suddenly he yanked my shorts and panties down. I was able to slip out of his grasp long enough to pull them back up but before I could make another move he was on me again. Pushing me and trying to trap me in the corner so that I couldn't get away, but I wouldn't stop trying to get away from him.

I couldn't figure out exactly why he was attacking me. I knew I didn't do anything wrong, or anything to make him angry, he just started attacking me out of nowhere. I was hurt that my friend was trying to harm me, and still was hoping that he was just playing and that any moment, he would stop, realizing that this joke had gone too far and he was scaring me. Then he would apologize to me and get me my soda and we would go back outside and start another tournament.

I began to scream but there was no one home to hear me and at this point he became angry. He grabbed me by my throat and shoved me against the roll of carpet so hard that he nearly knocked all of the wind out of me and I felt a bolt of pain shoot down my legs. He began squeezing my throat cutting off my air just enough to let me know that this wasn't a game. I began to cry, I told him he was really hurting me and I didn't want anything to drink anymore; I just wanted to go home. He never answered me. He just continued choking me. He squeezed my throat again, choking the words off in mid-sentence and I knew not to utter another word. It was in this moment that I realized that I was really in trouble and that he was going to hurt me and there was no one around to stop him. I never felt so alone in my life and I didn't understand why my friend was trying to hurt me. I stood there struggling to breath, my back was killing me and I was terrified, I didn't know what was going to happen next.

He held me there against the carpet for a moment and all I could hear was his breathing. He was close enough for me to feel his breath on my face. Once again he pulled my shorts and panties down and pressed his body against mine, sandwiching me between him and the carpet roll. He was so close that I could feel his mustache brush against my face. Then I heard his belt buckle clink as it came unfastened, then his zipper. He pressed his knee between mine until my legs parted, and my world went black. I still

I don't remember anything else that happened that day from that moment on, but what I do remember is this, I never viewed the world the same again.

Martin continued to sexually abuse me, for the next two years, and it happened daily during the week. He would call me when he was on his way over and tell me what to wear. He would enter my house through those storm doors just beneath my bedroom window. I watched as he crossed through Steve's back yard to enter into my yard. I would sit on my bed, dressed in whatever he had me wear, as I watched him open those doors and enter into my basement.

I was filled with shame, fear and hate all at the same time, knowing for the next thirty minutes or so, I would have to lay with him on that dirty blanket, spread out on that hard cold floor. Once he entered the basement, he would stand at the foot of the stairs and call me, when I opened the basement door, it was so dark that it took a moment for my eyes to adjust, and then I could see those gold rimmed glasses, and I would begin my descension down the stairs into the darkness where he was waiting for me.

Every time he left my basement, he would go home and call me. He always wanted to know details about what happened. He would always ask if there was anything white in my panties and I always lied and told him no. I didn't know what it was until later when I became a teenager and we had a sex education class in school. I don't know why I lied about it, maybe I didn't want to give him anything else; he had taken enough from me.

Thinking back, I can't imagine that no one saw this teenage boy entering my house on a daily bases. My neighbors were always coming over and letting my mom know what friends I had over and what I was doing outside. But this they missed? No one saw anything? Or did they just choose not to get involved? These questions haunted me for decades. I couldn't help but believe that if someone said something to my mom or to me, that the secret would have been broken, Martin would have been stopped, and I would have gotten the help I needed then, instead of twenty-seven years later.

Because of that dark summer day, and the years of abuse that followed, I was forever changed. The bright light that once shone in my eyes had been extinguished, and all I could see was the darkness in the world. The confident little girl, who loved life, was now a little girl filled with self-loathing and fear of what the world really was. An unsafe place for children, a world where people pretend to be your friend only to turn around and hurt you in the worse possible way, a world, that I didn't want to be a part of any more.

After that day, I thought about suicide daily and only found a reprieve from the realities of my life by immersing myself in a fantasy world where only good things happened to me, where everyone was nice to me and all of my friends could be trusted, because I had created them. I can remember that I would miss chunks of time, because I had retreated into this wonderful world that I had created. My grades at school suffered because all day I was in my fantasy world and didn't hear about assignments or upcoming tests or quizzes. As time went on, it became easier to escape into that world, and eventually I spent more time there than I did here and that was all right with me.

I didn't tell anyone what was happening to me because I was so ashamed. I thought that I would be blamed for what was happening and I think that would have been more damaging to me than the abuse itself. So I didn't tell, and the abuse continued, and my fantasy world became more important to me than anything else. It was more than just my safe place; it was the only place where I felt safe and accepted.

One day I found a porn magazine in my brother's room while I was being nosey going through his stuff. This was the beginning of my addiction to pornography. It was in the porn magazines that I learned about what was done to me in the basement by Martin. Those magazines gave me the words that described what he was doing to me. The only information about sex, back then, was porn magazines, so that is where I got my graphic information about sex.

Looking at porn magazines came second only to my fantasy world. I am sure if adults heard me talking about sex, back then, they would have wondered where I got my information. Today, a child with advanced knowledge of sex, especially of the opposite sex, anatomy and sexual positions, is a red flag that screams abuse and would result in the Division of Family and Children Services and counselors getting involved.

# 3

## *THIS HOUSE*

*This house had a secret that it never told. It was about a little girl who was just nine years old. You see some naughty things happened in this little old home, and her pain rose through the floor boards in the form of a moan. A monster came to her disguised as a friend and he did so much damage I don't think she can mend. Monsters like these commit a terrible crime and the wounds that they cause don't heal over time.*

*The pain and the suffering that this young girl felt was a million times worse than being hit with a belt. Her terror emanates from somewhere deep inside and is forever locked away in this young girls mind. He visits her often and contacts her by phone; he knows just what time this little girl gets home. He lies her down she is confused and dizzy, the monster stands over her preparing to get busy. He teaches her things little girls should not know and he coaches and directs her as if in a show.*

Two years after the abuse started, a new family had moved in next door. There were three teenage boys, Benjamin, Anthony and Trevor and two girls, Carla, who was sixteen and Karen who was 12. The Wrights, which was their last name, were very familiar with the Gravestown police. All of the boys had been arrested and spent time in juvenile detention at some point. Their older sister's boyfriend lived with them. All of them drank beer and wine and smoked weed and cigarettes, except Karen.

Karen and I became best friends, but I never told her what Martin was doing to me. I had made a promise to myself to never tell anyone what was happening because they would use it against me. Although our friendship didn't make me trust again, it did however introduce me to a very different world. When I started hanging out with Karen, my mother told me that her family was trouble.

Even though my mother knew that the Wrights were trouble, I knew she felt bad for Karen and she didn't blame her for her family. She did caution me about hanging out with her at her house. Karen and I started hanging out every day. I started wearing khaki pants, with a white shirt and a blue bandanna just like she wore. I tried to wear my hair like hers, with her baby hair smoothed down, but I didn't have any baby hair, in fact I hardly had edges.

33

One day we walked about ten miles to this park that was in an area that we would call the hood today. Most of the people there were wearing the same clothes as us. We went to several different houses and sat and talked with these older guys who were drinking beer, smoking and doing drugs. I remember feeling scared and excited at the same time. Looking back, I realize that anything could have happened to us. These guys who we visited were a lot older than we were, but no one ever did anything inappropriate.

I was eleven when I became friends with Karen. We both smoked cigarettes and we were spending a lot of time in the Glenn, as they called it. During this time, I lost contact, with all of my old friends and ended up making new ones. One day, Karen and I missed the bus to school and it was too cold to walk, so Karen's brother Benjamin said he would call a cab and take us to school. Karen and I lit up some cigarettes while we waited for him to get dressed.

When Benjamin came down stairs he lit up a joint, took a drag, inhaled it and blew the smoke at us. Then he handed it to Karen. She looked at me and then she took a drag, then she handed it to me. I didn't want Benjamin to think I was a baby, so I took a drag too! We passed it around until it was gone and by then the cab was outside and we left for school. By the time I got in the cab, I was high as a kite and couldn't stop laughing.

I was in sixth grade, and it was Iowa Test day at school. I remember the teacher asking me why my eyes were so red. I told her that I had a bad headache. Some of my classmates knew I was high and were whispering pot girl and laughing, which caused me to laugh uncontrollably. Weed made me feel wonderful! I didn't have a flash back, I didn't go to my fantasy world, and I didn't think about Martin or what he was doing to me the entire day.

I had found a way to escape that world and I enjoyed my new friends. I was surrounded by what I considered really tough people and I felt safe when I was with them. Looking back, I understand how some kids get drawn in by gangs. It is a close-knit friendship, and everyone has something they are dealing with, and you know that you are in with the toughest people around, and they are not going to let anyone hurt you.

After a few months, my life became more difficult. I was trying to live in that world, and still be a good student who was home on time and stayed out of trouble. It was worth the trouble though, because it was exciting and fun. Most of all, it limited Martin's access to me because I was coming home late from school and I was always with Karen. He still managed to have visits, but not as often as he used to.

I had my first tough girl test when Karen took me to Donna's house after school one day. Donna was really fat, and she used her weight as a weapon. She was the worst bully in school and everyone was afraid of her. She had her crew of friends and they terrorized the other students daily. No one told on her because they were afraid of what she would do to them if she found out they snitched.

When we got to Donna's house, it was like a party. Everyone was smoking cigarettes, weed, and drinking beer and wine and they were listening to music and laughing. It seemed like everything stopped when Donna saw me walk into the room. She stood up and in a low growl, asked Karen what I was doing there. Karen told her I was cool, funny and could fight. Donna walked over to me and got right in my face and just stood there. I leaned in a bit closer, and stared her down until she took a few steps back.

I don't know what she saw, but whatever it was, she backed up off of me, laughed, and handed me a joint and a bottle of Old English 800, and said you better make me laugh too. That was it, I was in, with the toughest girls in school. For the first time I drank alcohol. I didn't like the taste of beer at all, but I had to drink it because I wanted to be cool like everyone else. Then someone passed me a bottle of Wild Irish Rose wine and I really liked it. That was my drink for the rest of the afternoon.

I sat with them for hours smoking, drinking beer and wine and making them laugh. Soon we realized how hungry we were. Donna went into the kitchen and found some Mrs. Smith fish sticks in the freezer and fried up two boxes. Karen and I chopped up onions and put all of it

together on white bread with mustard. It tasted so good. You would have thought we were eating lobster, but we were just really high and really drunk.

I was with my new friends every day. We would stand outside of liquor stores asking people to buy beer and wine for us. We always found someone willing to take our money and purchase what we asked for. We would then go to someone's house and get high. We would sober up, hitchhike home, and I would do my homework before my mom got home.

After a while, things started to get scary. Donna and her girls started getting arrested and each time they did, I was supposed to be with them but each time my mother told me I couldn't go with them. She would take me to the event instead of allowing me to walk with Karen. Seeing where these friendships were leading, I started distancing myself from the group. A few months later, Mr. and Mrs. Wright broke up and they moved away and Martin's visits, picked up right where they left off. I was back in that dark pit.

At the beginning of the summer, before I started eighth grade, I was home alone. I was looking for matches or a lighter so I could smoke. I couldn't find one, so I went into the kitchen and lit it off of the gas stove. I opened the back door to let my dog out not realizing that I had left the burner on after I lit my cigarette. Our back door was in the kitchen, and the stove was too big for the space, so the back door would hit the stove when you opened it.

While I was sitting on my bed smoking and watching my dog walk around the yard, I heard glass break. I ran into the kitchen to find that the back door curtain had caught on fire, burned the door and broke the window. I panicked! How was I going to explain to my mother what happened? I ran through the house crying and trying to figure out what to do to get out of this. I knew that my mother was going to kill me when she found out that I was smoking and as a result I almost burned the house down.

Then I got an idea! I went into my mother's room and

pulled out all of her dresser drawers and scattered all of the contents all over the room. Then I ran to the living room and took the mail and threw it all over the living room. I called my mom's job. When the secretary answered, I was hysterical, and the secretary knew I was in trouble. I could hear her running through the office calling my mother's name. I knew at this point that there was no turning back now; I was in it to the end.

When my mother came to the phone, she could barely understand what I was saying. All she could make out was that Martin had broken into the house and tried to get me and then set the kitchen door on fire. My mother made it home in record time. She had a good friend of the family, Mr. Lee, come to the house while she was on the way. He didn't live far. By the time it was all over, the house was full of police and they were making a report.

I could tell that the police didn't believe me, because they kept asking me, are you sure this is what happened? I stuck to my story and kept saying "Yes!" One officer asked if I was in the house while Martin was there. I told him yes. I told him that I was hiding in my mother's closet. I don't know what the police found out about Martin, but within a week of that incident, his whole family packed up one night and moved out.

A lot of things happened that summer. After Martin left, I began playing basketball with the sparks boys that lived at the top of the hill. After a few weeks, Michael Sparks and I had a crush on each other. Right around this time, my mother had started taking me to the salon with her to get my hair done, and when I would get home, I would rush up the hill, not to play basketball, but to watch Michael play. In between games, he would come over and sit so close to me that our legs touched. I was in heaven!

The next time that I had come home from the salon, I was heading for the front door, when I heard my brother crying and telling my mother that there is no God. My mother was asking him what was wrong. Right when I had opened the front door to leave, I heard him say, "One of the Sparks is dead." I froze in my tracks and I turned around and asked him, "Which of the Sparks brothers died?" I knew two of the older brothers were his best friends and they were always together. He continued to cry and I asked him again, "Which of the Sparks brothers died?"

My mother managed to get him to the couch to sit long enough to tell us what happened. Michael Sparks drowned. As my mother consoled my brother, I walked to my room, laid on my bed and cried. No one knew that he and I liked each other, and that he was the reason I was

40

keeping my hair nice and going to watch him play basketball instead of playing myself. I remember thinking that I was somehow responsible for what happened because of what happened between Martin and me.

I spent the rest of the day in my room, and the rest of the weekend in the house. After I received that news, I didn't go out much. Any joy that came from Martin leaving the neighborhood was totally destroyed with the death of Michael. I was devastated, but instead of telling someone how I was feeling, I simply added him to my bag of secrets. So no one knew how much his death impacted me; how his death added to my dark view of life and the world.

After such a rough summer I was ready to start school. I reconnected with old friends. I tried out for, and made, every sports team including track. Steve and Todd were still my good friends, even though I didn't see Todd as often anymore. We were growing up and would be going to high school soon. During the last month of school, my mom wanted to meet with my sister and me to talk about something really important. I was so scared because I thought that they had found out about what Martin had been doing to me over the last three years.

That was the longest walk from the bus stop. All the way home I kept trying to figure out how they found out.

What was I going to say when they confronted me about it? When I got home, they were waiting for me in the living room. My mom said that she had some bad news to tell me and I wasn't going to like it. She went on to say that she had gotten a new position on her job, but it was in a different city. We would have to move away. "That would mean that you will be going to high school in a different town, away from your friends," she stated.

I remember the shock on both of their faces, when I jumped up and said, "That is great! When are we moving?" My mother said in a few weeks. "You're okay with this?" she asked. I emphatically said, "Yes! I am excited about moving." I went to my room, leaving my sister and my mom in a state of shock. I lay on the bed and rolled around giggling to myself. I was going to leave this house and all that happened here and start a new life, in a new city, going to a new school where I can meet new friends, and leave this life behind me.

During those few weeks before moving, I began packing up my room. While I was packing I was making plans, on how I was going to change when I got there. I promised myself that I wouldn't play any sports and that I would make friends with the girls. I would be a totally different person from who I am now. The time flew by, and before I knew it, I was pulling up in front of our new house. The only thing was, all of my issues, had packed up and moved with me.

I really thought that the flash backs I was having would stop when I left McLaren street, but they didn't. Unfortunately, they were intensified as my hormones kicked into full gear. I was constantly looking at porn magazines and I went to my fantasy world even more. When school started, it didn't take me long to meet people. Making friends came easy for me. When I got home from school, I would meet up with the girls in the neighborhood, and we would walk to the park because that was where all the boys were.

Our spot was sitting behind the fence on the tennis court where we could watch the boys play basketball. I usually missed most of the conversations, because I was so involved in watching the game and resisting the urge to ask if I could play. One day when we arrived at the park, Vanessa ran onto the court and stole the ball, interrupting their game. The guys were telling her to stop playing and give them back the ball, so they could finish their game of twenty-one. But she kept the ball and said, "I bet you we could beat you in a game." The boys laughed and accepted the challenge.

When she called all of us to get on the court, I hesitated, remembering my promise to myself. I remember thinking, "If I play, this is going to put you back on the outside." But the truth was I didn't like what was on the inside because I didn't fit there. When Robert saw me hesitate, he said, "Look at Stephanie, she is already scared and we haven't even started yet." All the boys and some of the girls started laughing, and that was all I needed to hear to persuade me to play.

The boys let us have the ball first. Vanessa, the one who started all of this, had to try to dribble the ball around the court instead of passing it. One of the boys took it easily. I was still playing the role, and I let one of the guys pass by me for a layup. Every time I got the ball I would throw it to one of the girls and one of the boys would steel it. The next time Vanessa got the ball, she threw it to me and when I turned around, Robert was in position to guard me.

Now I knew from watching Robert play that he was no match for me. He swiped at the ball, but I was too quick, and his teammates started teasing him. So he swiped at it again, but he wasn't fast enough. When I started dribbling, he tried to steal it, and I put the ball between my legs and took off for the basket for an easy layup. Everyone was surprised, but I just walked back to the foul line, and yelled, "Check!" When I did that, all the boys knew that I was a ball player. Surprisingly, the girls screamed with excitement and said, "Let's go girls!"

We played a good game. Every time one of the girls got the ball, they immediately looked to pass it to me. By the end of the game, they were making shots too. We lost, but the secret was out. As I walked off the court with the girls to sit on the tennis court in our usual spot, one of the guys yelled for me to stay and play some more. I looked over at the girls, who were looking at me, waiting to make a decision. I turned and went back to play ball with the guys.

All that week, the guys were trying to get me to try out for the basketball team. I wasn't sure I wanted to play. These girls are tall and really good. I had never played against girls who knew how to play. The competition was tough. That weekend my mother asked me if I was trying out for the basketball team and I told her no. When she asked me why, I told her that I was too short. She told me that I may be a small piece of leather, but I am put together! We both started laughing as she pretended to dribble around the kitchen.

When the week of tryouts came, I was there. The conditioning exercises were grueling. I had shin splints so bad, that I had to ace wrap both of my calves to get through the tryouts. I wasn't in the best of shape. Over the last few months I had picked up weight and I was still smoking, but I knew what I lacked in conditioning, I would make up for in my ball playing. When we scrimmaged, that was when I shinned.

On Friday, they put up the list of the girls who made the team. When I checked, my name wasn't on the list. I was really disappointed. This was the first time that I didn't make a team. I went to my locker and headed for the front door. When I opened the door, one of the girls who tried out, caught up with me. She said, "Congratulations for making the team." I told her I didn't make the team. She said, "Yes you did." I returned to the gym doors where the list was and realized that there were two lists- one for junior varsity and one for varsity. I was the only freshman to make the varsity team.

I was on cloud nine on the bus ride home. I couldn't wait to tell my mom, my brother and my sister the great news. That night while eating dinner, I told them what happened and they were all excited. Of course nobody doubted me for a moment, except me. While I was doing the dishes, I smiled to myself and said today was a really good day. I finished up the dishes and walked my sister out to her car; the stars seemed extra bright that night. When we got to her car door, I called her name, but when she turned to me, I just said, "Good night."

I was so close to telling her what happened to me, but instead I watched her pull out of the driveway and drive away, along with the opportunity for me to tell someone what I was going through. All though it was a great day, the undercurrent of depression was there waiting to wash away any happiness that I experienced. I went back into the house knowing what the night had in store for me.

The rest of my high school years were unremarkable. I didn't date, even though a few guys were interested in me. It was too complicated for me to date with the secret I was holding. Because I never told anyone, I didn't have anyone who could explain what happened, or correct any incorrect beliefs that I had about my role in what happened. So I just kept it simple, even though that meant missing out on all of the events that happened when you grow up and start dating. There was no first date, no junior prom and no senior prom.

After high school I did a few years in college, that were not successful. I then moved out of state to join my family. I started working for the phone company where my whole family worked. I got my own apartment and I continued to deal with my past as I had always done- by smoking weed occasionally and visiting my fantasy world daily. I worked for the phone company for about two years before I quit and moved two hours away to live with my sister.

# 4

## THE SEA

*Why has fate chosen me to cast out upon a lonely sea, a sea so full of pain and tears, and memories of some taken years.*

*How much longer can this go on, I am trying my best to weather this storm, but the skies are gray and the seas are high, sometimes I think I am going to die*

*Trying hard to stay afloat seems useless in the leaky boat, and the sharks are circling all around and I am just floating here nowhere bound.*

*Bound for nowhere that's the name of this game, and I know that I will never be the same, because when I look in to that cold black sea, all I see is a reflection of me.*

*That's my pain and my tears that have built up over so many years and has turned into a raging sea that is waiting here to swallow me.*

# I LET MY SOUL RUN FREE

I was twenty-seven when I moved in with my sister so that we could open a handbag shop in St. Augustine Florida. We opened on the day after Thanksgiving, after spending months getting suppliers, and shopping for high quality handbags to put into our store. During our first year of working the store, I started really having trouble dealing with the secret that I held since I was nine. On one of the days I was scheduled to open and close the store, there was hardly any business.

While sitting at the counter waiting for customers, I wrote *The Sea* poem. I became so overwhelmed with sadness that I couldn't finish out the day. I called my sister and told her I didn't feel well and that she needed to come and close the store. I got home in the quiet of the house and I cried. I felt that all the burdens of the world were on my shoulders. I knew I had to tell someone or I would go crazy. My heart hurt, my stomach was upset, and I had the worst headache I've had since high school when I was diagnosed with migraines.

At some point, I must have fallen asleep because the next thing I knew, my sister was waking me up asking if I had already eaten. I told her no and we both went into the kitchen to have dinner. When she sat down in the chair she looked at me with concern. I felt my eyes welling up with tears. She asked me what was wrong. You look like you have killed someone. I told her I couldn't tell her so I went upstairs to my room and wrote on a piece of notebook paper about Martin molesting me from the age of nine until I was thirteen.

When I finished the note, I went back down to the kitchen and gave it to her. After she read it, she looked heart broken. She stood up and hugged me and then she shared with me that both her and mom noticed the change in me. They even had a meeting to try and figure out what was going on with me. She said, "You started to wear jackets all the time, you were always in your room, and you just weren't the Stephanie we knew."

"We chalked it up to you going through puberty and trying to adjust to the changes that your body was going through. We never would have guessed that you were being molested. You know mom would have killed him if she knew, and you know I would have too," she said. We talked for a while before we went up to bed. Once in my room, I remember thinking, "The cat is out of the bag now." Even though I saw the pain in her eyes, I still thought that she would think less of me now that she knew what happened.

When I woke up the next morning, it was the first time in my life that I was afraid to face my sister. I was so full of shame and I felt like my soul was being torn from my body. I felt so bad putting this burden on her when she was already stressed over the new store and our financial situation. Now she had to worry about this. I was so angry with myself for not being able to handle this without bothering her.

Instead of my world getting a little bit lighter now that I shared the secret that had haunted me for so many years, my world got a whole lot darker. Every emotion that I had concerning this event was multiplied a hundred times and I didn't want to get out of bed, but I knew I was going to have to face her eventually. I showered and I got dressed and I went down stairs as if we didn't have a life changing conversation, but she wouldn't let that happen. She greeted me with a hug and told me how much she loved me. She told me that it was going to be alright.

When I talked to my sister during breakfast, I made her promise that she wouldn't tell mom. I didn't want her to be disappointed in me too. For me, the less people who knew, the better it was for me. I was so ashamed of what happened. I can't remember how much time had passed before my sister confessed, with tears in her eyes, that she had told mom about what happened. Before I could react, she told me that she had to tell her because I needed help and she couldn't afford to pay for the therapy; mom had been paying all this time.

She told me that mom was very upset because she was molested when she was a little girl, by the husband of the woman who took in her and her sisters when they were orphans. I cried for my mom because of what happened to her. I cried even harder because I know how difficult it had to have been for her to keep that secret. I know she wanted to grab her baby girl (me) and hold and comfort her during a time when she needed her the most. But as usual, she put her children first and she paid for my therapy and she never let on that she knew what happened to me back on McLaren Street.

No matter how hard I tried, I just couldn't get my footing. I couldn't find a place where I fit in. I was just going through the motions; my life had no meaning except to torture me daily with the flashbacks of the molestation. The flash backs didn't just happen when I slept, but when I was awake as well. Sometimes all it took was a certain smell, or a song from that time, or someone who looked like him, to instantly transport me back to that dark basement.

After a year or so, the mall that housed our store closed and my sister and I opened a clothing store not far from where the handbag shop was. As fulfilling as it was to be entrepreneurs, it was the hardest work we had ever done. We often woke up in the morning shaking; we called it the entrepreneurial shakes. Now that we both are in the medical field we have oft times wondered if we were suffering from some type of seizure due to prolonged sleep deprivation.

In 1988, the bottom dropped out for retail. Major chains were closing all over the country including Zayre, the anchor store in the shopping center where our store was located. Prior to our closing, sales dropped drastically when another clothing store opened one store down from ours. Everything in that store was a $1.99. If that wasn't enough, it snowed and we had to close for a day or two. Then a few months later, a hurricane was headed our way and we had to close for a few days

After that, my sister decided to close the store and cut our losses. We moved back to Jacksonville to the townhome that my mother owned. Now, we both had to figure out what we were going to do next. After talking about it, my sister said, "You've always wanted to be a paramedic. Why don't you look into doing that?" I did some research and found out I had to be an Emergency

Medical Technician (EMT) first. I started with the American Heart Association CPR class. I asked the instructor where I could go to become an EMT and he told me the local community college offers the classes.

When I finished the EMT class, I took the state exam and passed. I was hired by a private ambulance company. I worked six days a week while I attended the Paramedic class at night. At that time the Paramedic course offered at the local community college was a two-year program, and when you completed the course, you received a certificate and you had an Associate's Degree that covered most of the prerequisites needed if you decided to go on to be a Nurse or a Physician Assistant.

Once I got my Paramedic License, I was working two jobs. I worked in the emergency room of a level one-trauma center and I worked as a private ambulance that transported heart transplant patients, and patients who were scheduled for a heart cath. I did this for about two years while my sister attended the same school to become a Respiratory Therapist. Then I wanted to ride on a first response ambulance that responds to 911 calls. Where we lived though, you had to be a fire fighter in order to do that.

I remembered going to the Merchandise Mart in Atlanta, Georgia, when we had our stores. I also remembered how much my sister and I liked Atlanta, even though we both felt like country bumpkins because we were both still wearing our jerry curl hair do's. When we went to Lenox Square mall, everyone looked so chic. The next time my sister went to Atlanta to buy merchandise for the store, she got her hair done and bought a new outfit before she started shopping.

So when I heard about Grady EMS, who hired Paramedics who weren't fire fighters, and that they are the main company for responding to 911 calls in Atlanta, I started the application process. I drove to Atlanta and went to talk to some of the supervisors about how I go about applying. They told me that the odds were slim to none because I don't live in the metro Atlanta area even though I have a Georgia paramedic license.

I was a little discouraged because I have to live in Georgia to get hired, but I can't move to Georgia without a job. I remember calling my mom, and as usual she lifted my spirit with her pep talk. She told me that while I wait to hear from Grady, I should look around for some other places to work. I had decided I would stay at the hospital and go to Daytona to do the bridge program to go from being a medic to a nurse. During this time, my sister met a nice guy, got married and moved out.

I began painting the place. I put in a new ceiling fan in the living room all by myself. I was shopping around for new carpet, when I got a call from Grady EMS. They wanted me to come in for an interview the following week. I hung up and screamed and called my mother and sister about the good news. I made reservations at a hotel in Georgia, and began preparing for my trip. After the interview, a few days later, I got a call offering me a job. I gave the hospital and ambulances service my two-week notice and moved to Georgia.

The problem with moving was that when I moved, my issues moved with me. It wasn't long before I began to succumb to the depression that had been hovering over me like a dark cloud. It was easy for me to isolate myself because I lived alone and the nearest family was over four hours away. Although I had made some good friends, I was overcome with feelings of loneliness, and the flashbacks were coming more often. I turned to what worked when I was a kid, alcohol.

This is when I started to really decline. Whenever I was off, I drank and I spiraled quickly from there. Then the thoughts of suicide and the prayers for God to take me from this awful life I was living began. One day I responded to a trauma call at work. While on that call, I didn't make the right decisions on the treatment for that patient. THAT was the tipping point. I beat myself up over that call-unmercifully. The patient didn't die or anything, but I couldn't get past the fact that I had made a mistake.

I would try to rationalize that everyone makes mistakes, but my work ethic and being the best at any job I ever worked, was the only thing that was right in my life. When I was at work, I always exceeded what was expected of me. That is what my mom taught all of us. It was the one thing that kept me holding on, but that was gone. I began to hate my job. It was getting difficult for me to go in to work. One day at the end of my shift, I walked by an ambulance crew and over heard them talking about the pediatric hospital across the street hiring paramedics. That was perfect! I had previous pediatric experience and I was certified in Pediatric Advance Life Support.

I applied for the paramedic position in the ER and was hired. I was once again starting over and the change allowed me to forget what I was going through for a while, but my issues were always just below the surface. It was easy for them to break through and torment me at any moment. I had given up smoking cigarettes and weed a few years ago, and now booze had become my best friend.

Eventually, I went from drinking occasionally to drinking all day on my days off.

For me depression was a palatable thing. I could taste the sorrow that rose from within me and it kept me in a constant state of nausea but would never let me throw it up. It just lay there in the pit of my being like a cancerous tumor that was in no rush to kill me. Deep depression permeated every part of me both inside and out. Every life stressor became another extension that was attached to the depression.

Life stayed hard, but I stayed focused on work. I worked nights so that I wouldn't have to be home, because I was afraid of the night. I worked hard because that was the only thing that I would give myself praise for. That was the only place that I found my worth. I worked a lot to keep me from isolating myself from everyone and falling into that trap that always seemed to lead me to believe that suicide was the answer. I may not have made the best decisions, but at the time, it was the best that I could do.

In spite of all of this, I always seemed to find some small glimmer of hope that kept me going and kept me from making a fatal mistake. Something always pushed me to keep trying and to keep living until I began to fight to live and stopped begging to die. Once I began fighting to live, things began to change just enough that I was able to embrace the possibility that I could one day find happiness and joy.

This time that glimmer of hope came in the form of a much-loved dog who loved me when I couldn't love myself. Her perfectly timed whimper stopped me from swallowing a lethal amount of pills and way too much liquor. An action that set me on the road to recover what life had taken from me- my peace, my joy, and life itself. Therapy was the next step. I was anxious, nervous, and unsure, but I didn't let that stop me.

I called the number to the mental health office, that was on the back of my insurance card and a pleasant women's voice answered. She told me the department name and asked how she could help me. I wasn't sure what to say. I had so much I needed help with, so I just said I needed to talk to someone. She said the earliest appointment is next Tuesday and asked me if I would like that appointment? I said yes, knowing that I wouldn't live to keep that appointment.

We confirmed the date and time and ended the call. I immediately poured another drink and began planning what I was going to do with my dog tomorrow. "This time I am going to kill myself," I confessed. Five minutes later, my phone rang; it was the secretary of the mental health department. She called to tell me that she had an appointment for 9 a.m. tomorrow morning and asked if I could make it. I replied yes and we ended the call.

I don't know if she over looked that time slot or if it was something in my voice that gave me away. All I know is that I was grateful. I knew that I could make it until the morning. I went to the bathroom and stood in the mirror. I knew I had a long night ahead of me, but because I had an appointment in the morning that could possibly start me on the road to healing. I knew I could make it. So I took a deep breath and said to myself, "Let the journey begin."

# 5

## *MY JOURNEY*

*My journey to becoming whole has been a long one, the paths are crooked, covered with stones and they all seemed to be up hill. But every day I pick myself up, I look into a stormy sky and I venture on. My feet are blistered from the long walks, my back bowed from the weight of the burdens that I carry each day. There have been plenty of opportunities for me to leave this path and wander into the darkness never to be seen again, but every day, I start upon this path anew, hoping to find what has eluded me for so long.*

*Another day of hiking under my belt, and still my destination is nowhere in sight.*

*I am tired, hurt and angry. I decide to take a hot bath to sooth my troubled soul and as I sit here I begin to cry, I can't help but question how much further do I have to travel before I find what I have spent a lifetime searching for. I ready myself for bed, I lay my head down on a soft pillow and as I begin to drift off to sleep I can feel the tears drying on my cheeks.*

*The night has engulfed me and another day awaits.*

I drank myself to sleep and I woke up early the next morning hung over and tired, and very apprehensive about my first appointment. Before I left, I called my supervisor and told her I wouldn't be able to work tonight and I didn't know when I would be back. I explained that I couldn't talk about it right now. I apologized about the lack of information. She said, "Don't worry about it. Take all the time you need." She let me know that she would call me later to check on me and that I didn't have to tell her anything.

I hung up, showered and got dressed, fed and walked the dog and left for my appointment. By the time I arrived my anxiety level was through the roof, but I didn't let it stop me. When I entered the lobby of the mental health department, I was relieved that I was the only one there. I checked in and took a seat. My heart was beating so fast I could hear it but I didn't leave- even though everything in me was saying skip this appointment and let's go home. Just then the door opened and a lady called my name. When I stood up my legs buckled a little and I thought I was going to fall.

"Come on Stephanie you can do this," I said as I made sure I was steady before I began to walk. I followed the lady down the hall to an office at the end. It was cluttered with books and had a chair next to the desk where she sat. She introduced herself and then asked what she could help me with. I felt my eyes well up and I cried and cried and I couldn't stop. After a few minutes, she handed me some tissue and said, "I can't help you if you can't stop crying and tell me what is wrong."

I finally stopped crying long enough to tell her everything that happened to me. I explained that I didn't know what to do. She asked me if I was suicidal and I lied and told her no. I have worked in the medical field long enough to know not to say I was suicidal. I wanted help, not to be admitted to some psych ward. She felt comfortable with my answer. She told me about a therapist that is on staff that specializes in adult survivors of childhood sexual abuse.

She told me to make an appointment with her before I leave, then she said I am also going to prescribe Prozac for you so that you won't be so emotional while you are dealing with this. I told her I wasn't going to take it because I make jokes about people who take it. She told me I needed to get a better attitude about the medicine and the therapy if I wanted to get better. I accepted the prescription, knowing I wouldn't fill it.

I stopped at the front desk and made my appointment

and headed out the door. Down the hall I could see the pharmacy on the right. Reluctantly I went in to fill the prescription, knowing I wouldn't take the medicine. I waited for ten minutes and then the pharmacist called me to a window. When I got to the window, he asked me if I had ever taken this medicine before and I told him no. He said you can't drink alcohol while taking this medication and it takes about six weeks to start working.

I left the window laughing to myself. I had a handful of pills in my hand ready to kill myself less than twenty-four hours ago, and you give me a medication that won't start working until six weeks from now? I threw the bag containing the script into the passenger seat and drove to get a sub sandwich and some more rum and coke. I knew I wasn't going to make the six weeks. When I got home I put my food on a plate and poured myself a drink. I looked at the bag with the medication in it and took out the pill bottle.

I stared at the large capsules and then I opened the bottle and washed a pill down with the rum and coke. I was excited to start therapy with someone who specialized in adult survivors of childhood sexual abuse. I had never heard about this so I decided to surf the web to see what information I could find. I was astonished at the number of websites dealing with this subject.

I spent hours reading other people's stories and the kind of things they struggled with as adults. I found comfort in knowing that I wasn't the only one this happened to, but at the same time I was saddened to know so many people had been sexually abused as children. The numbers were staggering, the statistics unimaginable. How is it possible that so many people feel like they were all alone, like I did?

The one thing that stood out was the verbiage we all used. We all used the same words when describing our abuse and the impact that it had on our lives. Most of us had avoided getting pap smears. Most of us had abused either drugs or alcohol, or both at some point in our lives. We were either promiscuous or asexual. And all of us were depressed, lonely, scared and anxious about life.

At my first visit with Susan, we talked briefly about what happened to me, my drinking and why I wanted to kill myself. Then she asked me if I believed in a higher power, I said, "Yes-" even though I truly believed that I was too dirty for even God to love. She also asked me if I had been taking the antidepressants I was prescribed. Again I responded yes. She asked me if I was still drinking and I told her no.

We spent the last part of our session talking about my treatment plan. She arranged for me to go to a drug and alcohol treatment center to be evaluated because she was concerned about my drinking and I couldn't drink while doing The Program. She began to tell me about The Program, which was a specialized treatment that is similar to hypnosis, but much more effective. She said it had been very successful in the treatment of soldiers with PTSD and is now being used with rape victims and abuse survivors who also suffer from PTSD. She recommended that I read the book about this treatment before we begin using it.

Before we finished the session, I had to promise her that I wouldn't harm myself and that I would call the suicide hot line if I felt suicidal. She walked me to the front desk and I scheduled my next appointment with her and an appointment to go to the drug and alcohol treatment center for evaluation. On the way home, I stopped at the Barnes and Noble and purchased the book, The *Program*. I was really excited about this treatment and looked forward to reading the book. This was my first assignment and I was going to make sure that I completed it.

I was a little apprehensive about the drug and alcohol treatment. I knew I didn't have a drinking problem.

67

I had a flashback problem that I treated with alcohol because I didn't know another way. I knew that I had to go through this for me to do The Program. After resolving that issue, I looked in the review mirror and caught myself smiling. It had been a long time since I felt hopeful and I began to embrace the idea that I might one day come through all of this and find happiness.

Once I got home and took care of my dog, I began to read the book about the program I was about to start. The way the lady discovered *The Program* was very interesting. I was really drawn in by the many testimonies of the people who had gone through *The Program*. It all seemed very fascinating, yet a little unsettling and scary. The method that was used seemed simple but yielded amazing results for people who suffered from PTSD like me, so I was intrigued.

That following Monday evening, I went to the drug and alcohol treatment center for evaluation. The gentleman who came to the front desk to greet me introduced himself as Bruce. He took me to the back. We entered a small room with a lot of clutter. He apologized for the mess and he gave me a test to complete. He left the room and I began the test. He returned twenty minutes later as I was finishing.

We sat in silence while he looked over my answers and jotted down a few notes. He told me that based on the answers I provided, he recommended that I do a six-week drug and alcohol treatment plan.

At the time, I didn't think to question what he found, I just knew that this is what I had to do in order to do *The Program*, and so I agreed. I asked when I would start. He said tonight and then told me to follow him. We went into another part of the building and walked up to a counter that had a row of urine cups on it. He grabbed one, wrote my name on it with a sharpie and handed it to me.

He said that according to one of the answers on my test that I had not had a drink in over a week and I nodded in agreement. He said, "So we are going to start you off with a urine test. Every week when you come in, you will have to give us a urine sample. If it is dirty, we will address that at that time. If you can't urinate, it will be considered a dirty sample."

When I went into the bathroom, I stood there for a moment trying to digest everything that was happening and it hit me like a ton of bricks. I am in an outpatient treatment center for drugs and alcohol. I had to resist the urge to walk out because I didn't have to do this if I didn't want to, but I wanted to get better. So I peed in the cup, washed my hands, and went out and gave my sample to Bruce. He gave it to another employee for processing and we proceeded down the hall to a large conference room.

There were about eight people already seated. Bruce motioned for me to sit down, and then he left. I found a seat in the center of the room and sat down. Within minutes people started introducing themselves to me. There was a doctor, a teacher, a pilot, and several other occupations, including me, the paramedic. I had to catch myself from being judgmental about the people I was meeting, because I was doing the same treatment plan as them.

A few minutes later the meeting started. We were given a brief summary about what to expect, their expectations of us, and the rules. We were then split up into small groups and put into a smaller room with one counselor. Bruce was the counselor of our group. We started by introducing ourselves and telling the group why we were there. All of the people in my group either had an alcohol problem or a marijuana problem; no heavy drug users in our group.

What we lacked in hard core drug users, we made up for with denial. There was the grandmother who insisted that she didn't drink alcohol, just beer. Then there was the weed smoker who believed it wasn't possible to get addicted to weed, and was just here because the court said if he didn't come he was going to jail. No matter how many times I told myself that I was here because of my drinking problem, I couldn't accept that. I knew I didn't have a drinking problem because I would sometimes go a week, maybe two, without a drink- no withdrawal symptoms and no cravings.

It was only when I was having flashbacks that I drank and over this last couple of months, that had increased a lot. The small group meeting lasted an hour. It was almost 9:00 pm and I was starving. When I exited the building, the only cars that remained in the dark parking lot were the cars that belonged to the people in the treatment center. I found my car and headed home to eat dinner and watch a movie.

After taking a shower, I made a sandwich, grabbed some chips and a Pepsi and settled down on the couch to eat. While I sat there eating, I went over the events of the last couple of months, up to and including today and I realized just how much I had been going through. No one knew what had been going on in my life. I finished off my sandwich, and instead of turning on the T.V. I picked up the phone and called my sister.

The phone rang four times. Just when I was about to hang up, I heard my sister say, "Hey kiddo! I was just thinking about you." When I tried to talk, I began crying. I could hear the concern in her voice when she asked me what was wrong. I told her that over the last couple of months I had been struggling with the abuse issues. I let her know that I started therapy, I hadn't been to work in three weeks, and now I am in a drug and alcohol program.

She listened to me ramble on and then she said, "I will be there in two days to see you." Even though I tried to convince her that she didn't need to come, that I wasn't as bad as I sound, she insisted on coming. We talked for a while about how she and her husband were planning to move here now that they had a child. She said I will talk to my husband about moving up there sooner, even if it means I have to come by myself for a few months to look for a place to stay. Although I felt bad about her having to make that long trip on short notice, I was glad she was coming.

My sister came as promised and I enjoyed having her here for five days. Before she left, she told me that she discussed moving here sooner, with her husband and he agreed. I know how her husband is about her being away from him for too long, and I asked her how she convinced him to go along with her plan. She said, I told him I had to get up there because my sister is in trouble, and he immediately agreed.

After she left, the loneliness set back in. I decided to settle down on the floor in the living room to give some much needed attention to my dog. As soon as I got down there, Stormy came running over licking my face and trying to lie in my lap. I had to keep pushing her off of me because she was too heavy. Finally she settled for laying her head on my lap so that I could pet it. We stayed that way until my back said it was enough and I got up and sat on the couch. She was a great dog and she always lifted my spirits.

The next five weeks went by pretty fast, and during that time, I finished the book that was assigned to me. I completed the drug and alcohol treatment plan. At our last meeting, we were given certificates of completion, which would never be hung in my house. We were given back our tests that we had taken on the first day. I was surprised to see that I had not gotten a score that indicated that I needed to be here. When I asked Bruce about it, he had a hard time explaining it to me.

On my way home I became angry that Bruce had me go through this treatment program when the test that they use to determine if someone is in need of the program, clearly showed that I didn't. As if I didn't have enough issues already- I didn't need the label of alcoholic to add to the growing list of mental health issues that I had. I waited until my next session with Susan and I told her about the test, and she said it must have been the reason why I was drinking that made them feel I needed to complete the treatment plan.

Although those six weeks went by fast, Susan and I made a lot of progress in sorting through my memories and feelings about the abuse. After several sessions, where I shared all that happened to me, except the fantasy world that I was not ready to share, she gave me a series of homework assignments for me to do. Then a session was set up for us to do a practice run of The Program, on a benign memory.

I was anxious to get started but a little nervous about what was going to happen, but I knew I had to do it if I was going to heal. It was time for me to face what happened, so that I can resolve it and get on with my life. On the day that we were going to try out The Program, I was pretty nervous and when she called me to the back, my heart started pounding, but I got up and followed her to her office. I sat in a comfortable chair across from her and she began asking me about how my week went.

After telling her all about my week, she asked me if I had thought of a benign memory that we can use today with the program. I told her I did, then I made myself comfortable and I told her I was ready. She explained to me what she would be doing. We talked about rating the memories and having a safe place to go when things got bad. This was no problem for me, so I began. She started doing alternating tap; I closed my eyes and tried to relax and follow the tapping. She then asked me to concentrate on the memory and I started thinking about the time when my babysitter's husband came home from work and beat her.

Suddenly I was back on Maple Ave, upstairs with Mrs. Hall, who was my babysitter. I was standing to the side looking at Mrs. Hall talk on the phone. Little Stephanie, who was five years old, was standing in the chair across from her eating a snack. I was able to see everything I was wearing that day, the color of the Formica kitchen table and chairs and I could smell the pork rinds that Mrs. Hall was eating.

Suddenly I was back in the office with Susan. She asked me what was happening. I told her that Mr. Hall was coming up the back stairs. She asked me if I needed to go to my safe place. I told her no. I closed my eyes again and followed the sounds of the alternating taps. I was back in the kitchen. I looked at Little Stephanie and could see the excitement in her eyes when she heard him coming. Then I remembered how much I loved him. He would gather me up in is arms and tickle me until I almost wet myself.

The door flew open and Mr. Hall stepped through the door. He was a tall man, who wore a navy blue button down shirt with matching pants and boots-the kind mechanics wear. When he stepped into the kitchen, Little Stephanie froze, and so did I. It was clear to Susan that I was frightened. She asked if I needed to go to my safe place. I told her yes. We stopped for a few minutes while I went to my safe place.

After a few minutes we continued with the memory. It only took a couple of taps before I was right back in that kitchen. I could tell Little Stephanie knew that something was different about Mr. Hall today. His eyes were so red and he was really mad. His booming voice filled the kitchen as he screamed at his wife for being on the phone. He was yelling and cursing at her. He ripped the phone out of the wall and threw it at her. Little Stephanie was still standing in the chair, but she was pressed up against the wall.

I remembered that while he was yelling, I was trying to become a part of the wall so that he couldn't see me. He stood there for a minute, not saying anything, just staring at his wife as she tried to calm him down. She was backing away. He looked at Little Stephanie, and in a low growl said, "Stephanie, go into the bedroom and don't come out until I tell you to." As I watched Little Stephanie jump down from the chair, I realized that I had backed myself against the wall too. The terror that I felt that day came back and I was frozen.

Hearing Little Stephanie's feet hit the floor when she jumped down out of the chair, snapped me back. I followed her into the next room. As we went through the living room, memories of dancing and playing with the Hall's children came back to me. I remembered how much fun my brother and I had playing in this three-story house on Maple Ave. I followed Little Stephanie into the bedroom and watched her shut and lock the door. She sat on the bed and didn't move, except for her shaking.

We were both startled by the sound of a scream. Back in the therapist office I was gripping the chair arms. Susan asked me what was happening. I told her how he sent me to the room, and I was sitting on the bed next to Little Stephanie. We can hear Mrs. Hall screaming and crying just outside the door. I told Susan that they were in the living room now. I told her that back then I was afraid because they were so close to the door.

I was looking at the door so intensely and listening to her screams that I didn't notice that Little Stephanie had moved to the floor behind the bed and was sitting there with her eyes wide open and tears streaming down her face. When I turned back to the door, I heard the phone ring. I must have made a motion with my head, because Susan asked me what was happening. I told her that I had forgotten about the phone outside the door. It's ringing.

Little Stephanie reappeared next to me. She put her hand on the door knob as if she were going to open the door. She pulled her hand back when the screaming stopped. Now all we could hear was the sound of his fists hitting her. I remember that it was at that point that I thought she was dying. Little Stephanie ran back behind the bed and sat down holding her knees and watching the door. I stepped back too, not wanting to hear that sick hollow sound of him striking her over and over again. As I stood there listening to him beat her, I remembered that while we lived there, many nights I would be awakened by the sound of people talking.

I would sneak out of my room and peek into the

living room where my mom would be holding Mrs. Hall who was bloody. The living room would be lit up with the lights from the police cars in front of the house. At the time, I didn't know what happened to her. I didn't understand why she was bloodied. I was brought back from that memory to the current memory by a loud knock on the door by the police.

My mind reeled as I was trying to grasp how this was all happening; it was like I was on some type of mind-altering drug as I narrated everything that was happening while Susan continued to tap. The sound of the knocking caused me to step back behind the bed too. I looked over at Little Stephanie and I remembered that I didn't answer the door because Mr. Hall said not to come out until he said so. There was more knocking. This time it was the lady who lived next door who was teaching me how to play the piano.

Little Stephanie stayed where she was and never said a word. She just sat there watching the door, terrified that at any moment, all of those people in the living room were going to crash through the door and beat her too. She just sat there crying with her mouth gaped open, silently screaming. The memory of that day was so vivid and so real that I began to cry also. Quite a bit of time passed;

Little Stephanie had stopped crying and started to fall asleep.

Then we heard a soft knock on the door and a familiar voice calling me. "Stephanie, it's me, mommy. Open the door sweetheart, its ok!" They had to call my mother home from work to get me out of that room that day. I remember running and opening that door and jumping into my mother's arms, knowing that I was safe now. As I sat there in Susan's office, tears began to run from my eyes, which were still closed.

She asked me what was happening now. I told her that I am standing in front of Little Stephanie. I told her I know that when my mother looked me in the eyes that day, that she saw the damage that was done. I was broken. I don't remember anyone ever talking to me about what happened that day. I know my mother managed to buy a house not long after that and we packed up and moved to our first house.

After a few minutes in my safe place, I opened my eyes and looked at Susan. She asked me if I was alright and I told her I was. She said, "Did anything that you witnessed change your feelings about what happened that day." I told her, I didn't realize how much guilt I had been carrying about what happened that day. She asked me why I felt guilty. I told her it was because I didn't answer the phone. I later found out that it was the lady who lived next-door calling because she heard the screaming and knew I was there.

Susan then asked me how I felt now and do I still feel guilty? She also wanted to know if working through this memory changed how I felt about what happened that day. I took a few moments to think about what she was asking before I answered her. Then I told her that seeing how little I was I now realize that there was nothing I could do to help Mrs. Hall that day. I was just six years old, just a child.

Then she said, "Stephanie, this is not a benign memory! This would be very traumatic for an adult to experience and you were just a child." She allowed me to sit there quietly for another minute or so before she asked me how I felt about *The Program*. I told her I felt like I had taken some kind of hallucinogenic drug. After experiencing this, I don't think I want to work on any abuse memories. She asked why not, especially after seeing how it helped? I told her I don't want to go back and go through any of that again, it is too vivid and to real.

We closed out our session with her explaining to me that whatever happened is in your past and has already happened. You are just going back now to work through what has already happened so you can remove any negative associations that you have about what happened, so that it doesn't have such a profound impact on your life today. I just sat there listening to her; I was still trying to wrap my mind around what just happened.

I left her office and went up front to make another appointment. Susan had told me that she was going to be out of town for two weeks and she would see me when she got back. She also told me that if I needed anything, call the secretary and she could get me in to see the psychiatrist. I made my appointment for two weeks from that day and left. When I got home, I was mad that I had stopped drinking. If there was ever a time that I needed a drink it was right now.

I sat down on the couch and went over the totally bizarre and frightening experience I had doing *The Program*. I couldn't believe that I had not thought about that day before today. I can't do this with the abuse- it is too real. I was there in that moment as it was happening. I don't want to go back there ever and relive any of those experiences. I am afraid what it will do to me, and I don't think I can survive.

Over the next couple of days all I could do was think about *The Program* and how real it seemed. Hollywood couldn't write a movie scarier than what this treatment modality is capable of producing- my very own horror movie based on my life, staring me. I think I am going to have to sit this one out! I need to leave the past, right where it is, in the past. With the kind of affect that *The Program* is having on me, I can't see the benefit of going back.

A week before my next session with Susan, I talked to my sister and she agreed to come with me for support. I then made an appointment with the psychiatrist that saw me on my initial visit. When I got to her office she asked me how therapy was going and I told her about my apprehension about doing *The Program*. She told me to tell Susan about my concerns and why I didn't want to do it.

She asked me if the medicine was working and I told her it was. I was not as emotional as I was initially, but I hardly sleep any more. She told me that was one of the side effects of the medication and she prescribed me a sleeping pill to help me sleep. Before I left her office, she must have seen the fear on my face, because she told me to speak to Susan about my fear of using *The Program* on the abuse memories.

# 6

## MY WORLD

*My world is a dark place, a place without faces and
shadows are just out of sight.
My world is full of danger and I am full of anger but I am
afraid to turn on the light.
My world is full of shadows and they are always hungry
and they are constantly out on the prowl.
And on the darkest of nights, if you listen really closely,
you can hear their sick hungry growls.
In my world, you have to be careful, because pain can
come from anywhere. And if they catch you they will hold
you real tight and your soul from you they will tear.
So if you see me, enter this portal, don't you dare try to
follow me inside.
Because this is the world, the sick, ugly world, where a
little girl's heart came to die!*

Today is the day that I meet with Susan to go back in time to a memory that has both baffled and scared me. As I finished getting ready, I can hear my sister's car pull up in front of my apartment. I gathered my things and headed out to the car. My sister asked if I was ready and I lied and told her yes. When we pulled out of the driveway, I was glad that the medicine helped keep my emotions in check otherwise I would have been crying my eyes out. We arrived a few minutes early for my appointment, so I settled in a seat while my sister checked out the reading materials that were available on the coffee tables.

After ten minutes or so, the door opened to the back and Susan called for me. I was already scared and now I felt light-headed, but I proceeded to the back like nothing was wrong. I looked back at my sister and told her I would see her soon. When we entered her office, we talked about how things went with me since our last session. I lied and told her things were good. She then asked me how I felt about today's session, which would be dealing with the abuse. I told her that I was a little anxious- which was another lie.

She explained to me again, that nothing could hurt me, and that I had already lived through this and that it had already happened. I said to myself, "She doesn't know what my world is like. If she did, she wouldn't want to come inside." I got comfortable in my chair, closed my eyes and I took a deep breath. She asked me if I have a memory in mind that I would be concentrating on.

I said, "Yes I do." And then we began the session. I started concentrating on the memory and she began tapping. Tap, tap, tap, and with each tap I became more relaxed; tap, tap, tap; my eyes were following the sounds of the tapping, moving back and forth under my eyelids, tap, tap, tap. Then my hands began to grip the arms of the chair. Tap, tap, tap; "Where are you Stephanie?" Susan asked. Tap, tap, tap, I tell her I am in Martin's house with Little Stephanie. Tap, tap, tap; "Where are you in the house?" she continued. Tap, tap, tap; "We are in the living room." Tap, tap, tap.

My grip got even tighter and I started breathing faster. Susan continued the sequence of taps and with each tap I went deeper into the dark memory of that day. "What is happening Stephanie?" Tap, tap, tap; "He is taking Little Stephanie upstairs. I had never been upstairs before!" Tap, tap, tap; "Are you upstairs now?" Tap, tap, tap; "Yes. I am standing behind Little Stephanie in the doorway of a bedroom." Susan continued to tap then asked me where Martin was. "He is standing in the bedroom to my left at the foot of the bed," I replied.

Tap, tap, tap; "Tell me about this bedroom Stephanie." tap, tap, tap; I looked at Little Stephanie, she was staring straight ahead, so I followed her gaze. I told Susan that Little Stephanie was staring into the bathroom on the other side of the room where there was a light on. There is an uncovered light bulb, on a long wire and it is swinging back and forth. Tap, tap, tap; "Is there anything else?" Tap, tap, tap; "Yes. There is a bed in the middle of the room with a very large pile of clothes on it."

Tap, tap, tap; "What is Martin doing?" Tap, tap, tap; "He is just standing there looking at the pile of clothes on the bed." Tap, tap, tap; "Is he saying anything to you?" "No!" Tap, tap, tap. Suddenly Little Stephanie gasped and I felt like I couldn't breathe! Tap, tap, tap; "What is going on now?" Tap, tap, tap; "The pile of clothes…" tap, tap, tap; "What about the pile of clothes Stephanie?" Tap, tap, tap; "There is something not quite right about them!"

"I can see you are getting more afraid. Do you need to go to your safe place?" Tap, tap, tap; "There is something not right about those clothes!" Tap, tap, tap; Susan, stops the tapping because she can see that I am getting more and more afraid. She told me to go to my safe place, but I ignored her and continued to look at the pile of clothes on the bed. "Susan! I think there is someone else in the room with us!" Then I let out a short scream and she tried to get me to my safe place, but it was too late. I jumped up and had to run to the bathroom almost urinating on myself. I thought I was going to vomit.

When I got back to her office, I was still pretty shaken up so she gave me a minute to get it together before we started to talk. "Stephanie that was a very frightening experience you had. Do you remember anything else about those clothes? Did you see anyone else in the room?" I replied no to both questions. "What was it about the clothes that scared you?" It was a very large pile of clothes in the center of the bed; there were no sheets on the mattresses. Martin was just standing there staring at the clothes and he wasn't saying anything, it was almost as if he was scared too.

I don't know if something moved, or if I heard something, but all of the sudden I knew that it wasn't just Martin and I in that room that day. There was someone else there and someone was underneath that pile of clothes and someone was hiding in another area of the room, maybe the bathroom. Other than that, I don't know what happened, and I don't remember anything else that happened that day at all. "Do you have any idea or suspect who the other person or persons could have been?" "No!"

I have always wondered who turned on the light in the bathroom because it was still swinging when we entered the room. I don't think anyone could have gotten under the clothes that quickly without being heard or seen. "This is not the first time you have talked about not having memories after something traumatic happened. Do you go somewhere else, like to a place where you feel safe- like the safe place you go to when we do *The Program*?" I told her no, because whenever I went to my fantasy world I was aware that I went. In this situation the rest of the day is just gone.

"Have you ever heard of disassociation?" Susan asked. "No, what is that?" "It's when something so traumatic or so scary happens to you that your mind goes somewhere else to protect you from it." "Some people say that they are actually outside of their bodies, watching what is being done to them. Have you ever experienced anything like that?" "No, not during those days, but I did have something weird happen a few years ago while I was living in Jacksonville." Susan asked if I felt comfortable telling her about it.

I told her about the guy I met at my job and how we started going out. I told her that I really liked him. I remembered how great I felt about dating because I was

89

thirty, soon to be thirty-one and had never had a relationship before. Back then I wanted so much to be like other women. I told her that for most of my life I felt like I was on the outside of life looking in, but during that time, I felt like I was on the inside, no different from any other woman, and it felt great!

I knew that as a result of the abuse by Martin, what came easy for other women was very hard for me; I was so distrustful of everyone. I wouldn't let anyone get close to me, because I believed that when people find out details about you, they will use it to hurt you. I vowed never to be hurt like that again. I was very happy during that time, because when I went out with friends and they began to talk about their boyfriends, for once, I would have someone to talk about too, plus it felt good that someone was interested in me- someone who didn't see the dirt and the damage.

We went on a couple of dates. One day, while I was at his house, we were sitting on his couch watching the news and he started kissing me, over and over again, very passionately. Then something happened that I couldn't explain. "What happened?" Susan asked. All of a sudden I came back and I was just staring at him. He had this strange look on his face. He sat up and suggested that we cool out for a while and just watch TV. So I sat up and said ok and we watched a show for a while then I left and went home.

"What do you mean suddenly you came back?" Susan inquired. The only way I can describe what happened to me that day, was that I heard a sound like the sound the really old televisions used to make when you first turned them on- that static sound is what I heard. I didn't know I was gone until I came back and I don't know how long I was gone, or what happened during the time that I was gone. That is the best description I can give of what happened that day.

I told Susan that I saw him maybe one or two more times and then I realized that he wasn't good for me. Susan asked me why I felt he wasn't good for me. I told her I knew he wasn't from the first time we talked, but I was ignoring all the red flags that were setting off my alarms simply because I wanted a boyfriend. I remember her sitting there looking at me waiting for me to continue so I told her about the many red flags that he threw.

I told her about the first time we met. We were both at work. I had never seen him before because he worked in the basement. He came upstairs one night and we caught each other's eye. He came over to me and we talked for a few minutes. He asked me if he could walk me to my car when I got off. I said yes and sure enough as I was gathering up my stuff and about to clock out, he showed up with a big grin on his face. I clocked out while he waited. Everyone was grinning and whispering, and I enjoyed every bit of it.

I said good night to everyone and we walked out the back entrance and headed to the parking deck. Now when we got to my car we began to talk. I guess you could say that we were trying to get a feel for each other. Then he asked me how I felt about hitting? I looked at him and I told him that my aunt's husband came home wearing some clothes that another women bought him and she set the clothes on fire while he was wearing them. Those are the kinds of women in my family. So I guess the answer is, "I won't tolerate anyone hitting me."

That was flag number one. Flag number two came on our first date. He called and asked me to come see him play basketball at a gym not too far from his apartment. I said okay. He picked me up, but before heading to the gym, he stopped at his ex-wife's house to pick up his son. I was shocked when his ex-wife came out and it was one of my coworkers. "That was the second red flag?" Susan asked.

No. I told her that it was just awkward. We continued on to the gym, but when we arrived, he took me over to the bleachers so that I could sit down, and then he threw his sneakers at me and told me to lace them while he walked over to talk to his teammates. When he finally returned, he found those sneakers right where he threw them, still unlaced. He looked at me and I looked back at him and he smiled and kissed me on the cheek then he laced up his shoes and played. That was flag number two and it didn't stop there!

On another date, I was sitting in his living room waiting for him to get ready so that we could go get something to eat. When he came out of the bathroom he noticed that I had gotten my hair done. Out of nowhere, he announced that this would be the last time that I cut my hair. I started laughing and told him that my hair was my business and no one tells me how to wear it. Looking back, I now realize that I was in a very dangerous situation. I was in his house and he was a very big man and he obviously had a control issue.

Then on our final date, after the make out session date, we had a big argument. I remember seeing red I was so angry with him. Again, I was in a very dangerous situation- alone in an apartment with this big man that I only knew for a short period of time. I knew on some level that he was trying to control me, but I chose to ignore the danger signs. We didn't go out again after that, but a few weeks later, my coworker who was his ex-wife, shared with me that when she was married to this guy, he beat her all the time and she finally had to leave the state to get away from him.

I remembered how pissed I was, not because I was surprised that he beat women, but because she worked side by side with me, knew I was dating him and never thought to let me know what he did to her. Susan interrupted me at that point and said, "Regardless of the fact that your co-worker didn't warn you, you should have paid attention to those alarms that he was setting off." She followed up by saying she was glad that I got out of that relationship unharmed. Then she wanted to go back and talk about the date when we were making out.

"You said that when you came back, he had a strange look on his face, what did you mean by that?" After hearing that static sound I was just staring at him. I was not saying anything or moving, it was like I was frozen. "Did you have any alcohol or drugs while you were with him?" I told her no, and then I told her that I was surprised because according to his ex-wife, he was an alcoholic.

Then she wanted to know if he ever said what happened or if I said anything to him. "No!" I replied, "But I wish I had the where with all to have asked that question, but I was bewildered myself. I didn't understand what had just happened either. I remember driving home that night thinking, "What was that?" I wrestled with that experience for a couple of days and then I tucked it away and never talked about it again until today. "Does that sound like disassociation?" I asked.

She said yes it does, but she wanted to continue to talk about the abuse. "You never told me about how the abuse ended, are you up to discussing that today?" "Sure, it was during the summer right before I started eighth grade. I had accidently started a fire in the kitchen, and to avoid getting in trouble, I staged a break in and blamed it on Martin. I believe that the police found out something about him during their investigation because the whole family packed up and left that same week."

"Wow!" She said. That lie ended up removing him from your life. I agreed and we began wrapping things up. She told me that the next time we meet she wanted us to discuss how we were going to proceed with *The Program* and the memory we worked on that day. I remember thinking to myself, "You have got to be out of your mind if you think I am going to do this again." The last thing I want to do is revisit any of those memories, but especially that one.

I remember that after my sister drove me back to my apartment that day, I sat down in the living room and tried to digest everything that happened. I realized that when I left her office that day, I had yet another thing to add to my list of issues. Along with PTSD, severe depression, anxiety disorder, I now can add disassociation disorder. I was supposed to be getting better, but it seemed like I was constantly finding out new things that put more distance between me and healing.

If that wasn't enough, the next time I showed up for work, I had an email advising me that we were no longer going to be using this health insurance and would be using another HMO. My heart sunk. I immediately called to check and see if there was any way that I could continue to see my therapist and they said no. When I told Susan, she was just as upset as I was. She investigated ways that we could continue our sessions, but she didn't have any luck either.

I never got to do *The Program* again, and even though I was able to meet up with Susan, it wasn't in a therapy session. Instead we met at the local mall for lunch so she could check how I was doing but it wasn't a substitute for therapy or for the incest survivors group. Surprisingly, just after receiving the bad news about the change in my insurance coverage that ended my therapy, I met someone at work, who introduced me to a whole new way of life.

I became fully involved with the New Age movement. I didn't know that was what it was at the time. All I knew was that I was depressed and looking for a life line from anywhere to pull me out of this dark pit. It was getting harder and harder for me to hide all the pain that I was feeling, and act like nothing was wrong. One day I went to work and there was a new guy working with us and over the next couple of weeks, I noticed that he was always happy and was full of wisdom, and full of peace.

I really enjoyed talking with this man because he seemed to see something in me that no one else saw, including me. At the time, I was still dealing with my abuse issues, and this guy knew just what to say to reel me in. I was an easy target. As we walked through a tunnel, he told me that I was very smart and very influential. He went on to say that he noticed how people are drawn to me and how they listen when I speak. He asked me if I knew the good I could do and the changes in people's lives I could make.

I was hanging on his every word. I was fully enjoying the idea that someone thought I could be useful for something in this world. I asked him to give me the names of some books that would feed my spirit and my mind and the next time that we worked together he had a list of books for me. He told me that on the list there were a few really good books, but *Book number five,* would change my life. I skimmed the list and promised myself I would read them in order, but of course, I had to skip to *Book Number Five*.

# 7

## *ARE YOU AWAKE?*

*It boggles my mind that in this day and age I can be persecuted for my thoughts, ideas and the words that I speak, and it is amazing that I always run into obstacles when searching for the answers that I seek.*

*The people in power have made a large investment in ignorance and they label so-called undesirables a hindrance. In our society people who are intelligent are demeaned and made fun of, we call them nerds and geeks; we are constantly rewarding those who are strong in body and whose minds are weak.*

*Government policies are always changing and every day they introduce a new bill,*

*They are constantly asking us to choose between the red and the blue pill and each time we choose the same, believing it was of our own will.*

*But instead of fading into the shadows unnoticed, I am standing in the front of the line and giving notice, that I won't stand by quietly and not question your motives.*

*Knowing all this, I refuse to give up and join group think because I know that my quest for inner knowledge won't let the universal ship sink.*

*So for now I carry the burdens of those who are still sleep, Hoping that one day soon they will awaken and together we can do a clean sweep, So that when the time presents itself we can all make that quantum leap.*

*Until then, I will stand stoic and proud and I have no interest in being a part of the crowd.*

*And when I speak, it will no longer be in whispers but out in the open and out loud.*

*So, those who want to listen can hear me, and those who don't fear me will join me in the quest to find out who and what we really are.*

*Together our voices will make the earth quake, but first let me ask you this, are you ready? Are you sure you are awake?*

I wanted my life changing experience to happen as quick as possible, so that next afternoon, I went out to the nearest bookstore and brought a few of the books on the list, but I was only interested in the book that he said would change my life. I needed whatever was in that book and I needed it now. Before I even started to read it, I believed it was going to be my lifeline and that was something that I was desperately in need of.

During the time that I was reading this book, I started going to meetings with him and some other like-minded folks. Things really started looking up. I met other people who believed as we did. They would always tell me how bright I was, not mentally but spiritually. I took classes about crystals, learned about Chakras and started studying quantum physics and was shocked at how easily I understood it.

It was around the year 2000 when I was introduced to a new way of thinking. It was a breath of fresh air that breathed new life into me, or at least, that is what I believed it at the time. I was desperate for anything that would take away the depression that I had been living with all these years, and these new friends didn't judge me on how I dressed. They weren't concerned about who I was dating, or why I wasn't married, or why I didn't have any kids.

They just wanted to help me understand the power I had within me, and how I could learn to use that power to create the life I wanted.

Now, *Book Number Five* was everything that he said it would be. It was skillfully written. It captured me with the opening line of chapter one. Once I started reading it, I couldn't stop. I picked it up every chance I could, even if it were just for a few minutes. I would squeeze in a few sentences. That book had a profound effect on my life. I was more than changed; I was made new, by the writer's interpretation of the scriptures.

I thought I had found the answer to life itself and couldn't wait to tell everyone I could about this great book. I read part one, then part two, and part three. With each book, I became more convinced that this book was the truth. I read and re-read the first book, and then I went over it again. I was highlighting the main points and scriptures. After that, I went through it again and cross-referenced it to the Bible so that I could show people that this book came from the Bible.

There was such a change in me that people around me wanted to read it too. This book opened my mind up in such a way that I wanted to know everything and I believed I could learn anything. I went to the bookstore and picked up two books, one was *Alice in Quantum Land* by Robert Gilmore and the second was *Quantum Physics for Dummies* by Stephen Holzner. When I went to the register, the young man ringing me up made a comment about my choice of light reading as he put the books in the bag. I told him I just wanted to understand how the world works. Both he and my good friend, who was with me, chuckled at my statement and said, "Oh, is that all!"

I finished those books in no time and was teaching people around me about the basics of quantum physics. The man who introduced me to this new life, listened to me explain quantum physics and I could tell that he was amazed. He looked at me and said, "Who are you really?" That smile that he had on his face said it all! I told him that I was getting what the universe is trying to teach me, and I that I was just getting started.

I had begun to sleep in my bedroom again. This was something that I had not been able to do in decades. Not only was I sleeping in my room, but I was able to sleep without the lights or the TV on and with the door shut. I had stopped doing my nightly ritual of checking doors and windows several times a night and was able to sleep without flashbacks or bad memories or anything. I couldn't remember the last time I felt this happy. The next time I met up with Susan I told her everything that had happened and how my life had changed just by reading *Book Number Five.*

I remember how happy Susan was for me. She told me that she was going to go out and look for the book so that she could read it too. A few days later she called me at home to tell me that she went looking for the book that I told her about but she couldn't find it. Then she said as she went down the row of books one more time, *Book Number Five* fell off the shelf in front of her. I was beside myself with joy as I told her what happened is in line with how the book talks about how we create with our thoughts.

I started meeting other people who read the book and felt the same as I did. We began meeting up at each other's houses every couple of weeks. We were the seekers of the truth. The light workers! I was so excited that I wanted to write a book and I was going to call it *Free It Up!* I had a hard time starting it. When I talked about my writer's block with the gentleman who started me on this path, he suggested that I draw to open up my writing.

I told him I couldn't draw; he said just try it! I said, no seriously, I have trouble drawing a straight line with a ruler. He told me to go to the art supply store and get a pad and some charcoal and a blending stick and a cloth.

He went on to tell me how charcoal drawing is so forgiving, because if you make a mistake you simply wipe and blend it in and then start again. Then he said, make sure that when you are drawing that you clear your mind of everything and just draw.

It sounded crazy, but I did learn about quantum physics in one eight-hour shift at work.   I went to the art store and I got all of the supplies he told me to get and I bought a book with different drawings in it so I would have something to draw. I put on a CD of classical music that also changed your brain waves, and I started drawing. The first few drawings were awful, but once I cleared my mind, things changed.

By the third night I had drawn a picture that even surprised me. It was a picture of a man sitting on the ground leaning on a rock. He had a thick mustache, sunglasses and he was wearing a large hat and his arm was thrown over his bent knee. The details were almost perfect. Then I drew the picture of the Peacock with an elaborate feather design. I couldn't believe what I saw. I was actually doing charcoal drawings and they were really good.

I called my good friend and asked if I could come by and show her some drawings. I wanted to know what she thought. When I got to her house, I proudly laid the drawings on the table and waited for her reaction. She looked them over and said, "I want to be honest with you. I didn't expect anything really bad, but I didn't expect to see anything this good either, especially after you told me you still make stick figures."

I was so excited about my new found talent that I called my sister and arranged for us to have lunch the next day so she could see my drawings. When I told her about my drawings, she said, "You can't draw!" I said, "Yes I can!" "Well then, I can't wait to see them tomorrow," she joked. The next day when she picked me up for lunch, she came in to see the drawings that I had been bragging about. She was surprised at how good they were.

Over lunch we talked about all the changes that had been occurring in my life and by the time we were finished eating, she wanted to read *Book Number Five* too. She was happy that I was getting over my depression and sleeping in my room. She was relieved that I wasn't afraid of the dark anymore. Since she wanted to read *Book Number Five* to see what it was all about, I gave her one of my copies before she left to go home.

My writing opened up just like he said it would. The only thing I did differently was spend time drawing. Before I sat down to write, I would ask the universe for my story then I would open up my laptop and start typing. What came out was amazing. It was as if someone was dictating the story to me. I didn't even know what the next sentence would be. My fingers just played the keys on the keyboard like it were a piano and I was composing a beautiful symphony.

When I told people about my writing process, they couldn't believe that I didn't use an outline and that I simply sat down and started typing and a book came out. But that was exactly how I was writing. I would sit at the kitchen table, open my laptop and start typing. I would continue typing until it stopped. I would thank the universe for the story and stop for the day. I was just as amazed as everyone else. I started believing that I was a writer.

My life had finally changed for the better and it was becoming the best year of my life. I had not felt this good since I was a child. I continued reading *Book Number Five.* I continued drawing, writing and going to meetings with my new friends. However, time was flying and before I knew it the year was coming to an end. I began to feel sad until one morning I woke up reciting a poem. I quickly went to my laptop and wrote down the poem that had come to me in my sleep.

On New Year's Eve I went over to my sister's house to ring in the New Year. When I shared with her how great I felt, she cried and gave me a big hug and said she is so glad that I am happy and doing well. I gave her a copy of the poem I had written a few days earlier which made her cry even harder. She hung it on the wall in her living room and we went in the kitchen to prepare food for the New Year's celebration.

Later that night my sister and I were watching the ball drop in Times Square on TV. As they started counted down to ring in the New Year, I began to cry. When my sister saw that I was crying she came over and hugged me and asked me what was wrong? I told her this was such a great year for me. I didn't want it to end. She pulled me in her arms and said: "This year is going to be just as great. You wait and see." I dried my eyes and we toasted in the New Year with some sparkling cider. Afterwards, I headed back to my apartment.

While I was driving home I reflected back over my life and remembered where I started. Then I reflected back over the past year and tears started forming in my eyes again. It was so nice to feel good about myself and about my life, but I also had to be honest with myself, I was still longing for something. There was still a piece of the puzzle that was missing. I just couldn't figure out what it was. I shook off the feeling of emptiness that was infringing on my joy and concentrated on the road.

I drove the rest of the way home in silence as I contemplated where my life was heading next. Since I started my book a few months ago, I had not sat down to continue writing it. It is such a hard story to tell and I don't like going back to the darkest times of my life, but I had to in order to tell my story. I would often end up crying. I had been through so much and I don't even know how I was able to carry all those burdens by myself.

At that moment I thought of Susan and *The Program* therapy. Susan had mentioned trying to find a way to treat me so that we could finish what we started. I wasn't interested then, but maybe I would re-visit that suggestion. Maybe the key to this sordid mess that has imprisoned me for so long is hidden in my lost memories. Or maybe those memories weren't meant to be remembered at all. Only time will tell.

The New Year started off really great. I was on cloud nine until February, when my birthday came. For some reason this birthday brought up all the old stuff. I quickly sunk back into a funk. As I soaked in a hot tub, I could feel the thick curtain of depression descending on me and when

I couldn't shake the feeling, that the world was pressing in on me, and I felt like I couldn't breathe, I knew I had to do something right then.

So I picked up *Book Number Five* again and began to read it. I was trying to get back to that place I was in before today. One of my best friends had recently died of breast cancer and as I sat there soaking, I thought how unfair life was. She was taken when she had a husband and a young son and I am still here and had prayed for death. I could feel the grip of depression tightening and pulling me into the darkness.

Although the new age information kept me floating on cloud nine, there was always an undercurrent of sorrow that I couldn't shake. No matter how much I believed what I was reading, no matter how much better I felt and regardless of the book I was writing and my charcoal drawings, and my new friends; depression constantly fought its way back into my life and was trying to convince me that it was my best friend.

Sitting in that tub that night fighting off the feeling that I was sinking, I realized that I really didn't want to die. I just hadn't figured out a way for me to live yet, and I hadn't figured out how to go on with life while dealing with the issues that are plaguing me. What do I do when the drugs and alcohol no longer lessen or take away the pain? What do I do when family and friends get tired of my issues and fall away? What do I do when therapy is no longer an option or is no longer effective? This is when I simply feel like there is no other choice, for me, but to die.

But I refused to let myself loose the ground that I had made over the last year, so I picked up *Book Number Five* once again and began reading it from the first page. I got that same lift that I got the very first time I read it and I started to feel better with each turn of the page. I thought that this book was the answer to my emptiness and my depression and that I just needed to make a concentrated effort to read it more- that way the feelings of darkness wouldn't return.

The next day I was singing as I cleaned up the house and made lunch. My spirits were definitely lifted and I was convinced that I had *Book Number Five* to thank. I grabbed my lunch and took it to my room so that I could watch Oprah. After the intro, she informed her audience that this show might not be appropriate for children; the focus of the show was on pedophiles. I probably should have turned the channel and watched something else but I stayed tuned in. By the end of the show I was in tears and having flash backs.

This was a perfect example of how, given the right kind of setting, you can go from happy to having flashbacks when it comes to sexual abuse. I had not had a day this bad since before I started therapy. I didn't understand why I was slipping back to the old me, when I had weeks and months of great days. I started considering going back into therapy or joining a support group. I knew I needed to do something, because my boat was sinking and I don't know how to swim.

# 8

## *A lonely soldier*

*I look out every window, and check behind every door.*
*Searching for an enemy that I know is somewhere near, I*
*know this for a fact because my soul is full of fear.*
*I am just a lonely soldier I walk among the dead. The*
*faces that I see each night are swimming in my head.*
*I am battling with a force, that I just don't understand,*
*that's why I try to hide my soul deep within the sand. I am*
*just a lonely soldier, trying to find some peace. I am tired*
*of all this hiding it's time to face the beast. To find a place,*
*where I truly belong is what my heart desires.  But, I*
*can't seem to escape this place I am engulfed within its*
*fires.*

Later that day, after I got myself together long enough to think.   I began thinking about the time that Susan, after my fifty-minute hour, told me she wanted me to join the incest survivors group that she facilitated, because of the way my abuse affected me was so similar to incest survivors. She said that she had already asked the group if I could join them and they agreed. I told her I would think about it, and if I decided to come, I would meet her at the next meeting.

I remembered that I was a little hesitant about joining because I wasn't sure I was comfortable sharing what happened to me in a group setting.  After I joined, I realized, how much it helped me. Talking to other women who had been through the same thing I had been through, and were having the same feelings I was, really helped me in the healing process. Even though the abusive situations varied its effects on us were very similar

Looking back, I understand why Susan wanted me in that group.  The hurt and pain was not just from the sexual attack, it was the violation of my trust that seemed to do the most damage. When something like this happens, it leaves more than fluids on a sheet, or on a dusty quilt laid out on a cold hard floor in a dark basement. No, this burns through your heart and leaves a dirty stain on your soul and it becomes a constant reminder that trust equals pain and this is how I felt for the majority of my life.

Martin shook the very foundation upon which I lived; he took away my love of life and replaced it with mistrust and fear. Now I walk this earth a lonely soldier always ready for battle. Now I live in a world where everyone around me is a potential enemy. This is a lonely and frightening way to live, but it is the only life I know and within it I feel safe. Here it is almost forty years later and this man still affects my life. He doesn't hunt me anymore, now he just haunts me! His grasp and control of me has managed to span time and still exist in my life today.

What happened to me in the basement killed who I was and who I could have become. I remembered a few lines from a poem I wrote; every *time that he came to lay, he took another small part of me away. I wonder if anyone else can see that I am just a shell of who I used to be!* Sitting here after having such a hard day yesterday, I began thinking about the past 40 years, trying to understand why I can't beat this thing.

The after effects of the abuse radiated through my life like a crack in a windshield. It obscured my view of the world and my life felt like a huge puzzle that was missing all of the main pieces. I felt alone, even though family and friends surrounded me. I desperately wanted to be like everyone else. I was too scared to participate in life because the world was now a dangerous place.

This was my life and this is why I started calling myself a lonely soldier. It's me against the world, because I can't trust anyone else with my life, especially the details. So I stayed in my own little place in the world and I didn't let anyone in for fear that I would be hurt, and pain was something that I avoided even though it meant being extremely lonely and feeling like I was on the outside of life looking in.

I remember after my therapy was over feeling like a diver out at sea who had come up for air only to find that the boat had left. Now he was out in a vast sea all alone with no way to get back to land. Not wanting to drift back into that pit of despair, I started looking online for support groups to help me cover the rough spots that *Book Number Five* had missed. I couldn't think of anything else to do.

I sat down at the computer and typed, *support groups for adult survivors of childhood sexual abuse*, in the search engine. There were thousands of results. There were sexual abuse hotlines, male survivors, and Christian survivors, there were ritual abuse survivors, rape survivors, and the list went on and on. I didn't know that so many types of abuse existed. They had an online support group for each and every one of them.

Sitting behind that computer I realized that this wasn't something that was happening to a small percentage of the population, but met all of the qualifications of an epidemic. The amount of people that were affected by abuse was staggering. The consequences touched all facets of society. It transcended race, religion, gender, sexual orientation and economic status. Not one part of society was excluded from sexual abuse.

I sat there wondering how something this vast was not being addressed on a larger scale. I felt like there should be more congressional hearings on abuse, more task forces, protests in the streets and outside of the White House. American society is being overrun with predators that are severely damaging its citizens and causing an increase in crimes, drug and alcohol abuse, suicide, murder, and rape.

Sexual abuse produces more abusers, and they in turn produce more abusers and this cycle continues with no end in sight. How do we stop a train that is traveling at full speed through this world? It is stopping at every neighborhood in the world to pick up more victims.

The answer: by shining light on this dark subject, by exposing those who are committing these crimes, and by taking away the reasons for secrecy.

After losing several hours researching, I started going to individual websites to find a group that was going to work for me. I think it would have been more successful finding a group if I had never had group therapy. I missed the face-to-face interactions. Words without voices and faces cannot convey adequately the impact that sexual abuse has on a person's life. For me it was like being thirsty and drinking from an empty cup. I was tired of being alone and isolated and to me, this was not an adequate substitution for face-to-face interaction.

However, I did learn a lot about sexual abuse. One site identified the signs and symptoms of sexual abuse. When I read the list, I had just about every one of them. As a child I had become withdrawn, my grades dropped, low self-esteem, advanced knowledge of sexual behavior and language, excessive masturbation, suicidal ideations, change in how I felt about my body and the list went on and on. It was enlightening and at the same time depressing, hurtful, yet helpful.

We have access to vast amounts of resources on this subject, but we still haven't come anywhere near stopping sexual abuse from occurring. Instead of all of the new technology helping to tame this epidemic, it is used to make it easier to locate and abuse victims on a larger scale. Sexual abuse of children has become a high-tech, multimillion-dollar industry with no signs of slowing down.

Child abductions, child prostitution, and child murder has become so common and yet it is still so taboo to talk about. I am afraid society has become desensitized to it. It is something that definitely exists. We know how dangerous it is, but no one wants to talk about it, and no one wants to believe that it is happening in his or her neighborhood or in his or her house. Yet the evidence of its existence is all around us. It seems like every day we hear of missing children, children rapped, and children murdered.

In my spare time, I continued to do research trying to learn all I could about sexual abuse. I wanted to know about the characteristics of the perpetrators and the victims. I wanted to know what family dynamics prevented sexual abuse and which ones provided an atmosphere that was conducive to abuse occurring. I understood that the perpetrators are very careful and very clever when committing this crime.

As I combed through the information, I did not find a group to join, but I did learn a new word. When talking about pedophiles, the word grooming kept coming up. I decided to look up the word to find out exactly what it meant. Grooming is when someone builds an emotional connection with a child to gain their trust for the purposes of sexual abuse, sexual exploitation or trafficking.

I noticed that the only real training that was going on for the prevention of child sexual abuse was directed at helping children understanding the importance of telling their parents or someone they trust if someone is touching them. There is also the push to make sure parents, teachers and caregivers are able to recognize the signs and symptoms of sexual abuse.

I found both of these methods not only ineffective, but also unacceptable. The goal should be to prevent child sexual abuse; instead, we are being taught how to recognize the signs and to tell someone when it happens. At this point, the damage is already done. The child's life is damaged and the result is another link has been added to the cycle of abuse.

After reading up and becoming familiar with the dynamics of abuse and from my own experience, I realized that trying to teach a child not to trust someone just doesn't work. It seems that children instinctively trust people, especially those who are family and friends, and those who are policeman, teachers, priests and other adults that they come in contact with.

Then it dawned on me, what if we could find a way to teach kids and adults, how to recognize signs of the grooming process, so that they can talk to an adult about what they are experiencing. An adult could start a conversation with a child whom they think a predator is targeting. In order for child molesters to be successful, they not only have to groom the children, but the parents and caretakers as well.

Once they pick a child to victimize, they have to observe the child and the family. Then they start trying to gain their trust; this means the perpetrator has to spend quite a bit of time with the child. That should be the number one red flag for parents. You need to know why this person has taken such a big interest in your child. A few good hard questions might be enough to scare of the perpetrator.

In order for you to know who is around your child you have to be present in their day to day lives. You must pay attention to what they talk about, no matter how busy, tired or stressed you may be. The key to identifying a

121

groomer will show itself if you pay attention to what your children are saying. It is not enough to tell you children not to speak to strangers, because people stop being strangers the moment a person starts talking to a child.

Perpetrators know this and they use this to help gain their trust. Another tactic they use is they pay intense attention to the child. They make the child feel special, and they may buy them toys, or food, anything that will make the child want to spend time with them.

After the emotional connection is made, the perpetrator may begin to take the child on trips to the movies or to the park, to gain the trust of the parents and to spend time alone with the child. Then the secrets start-they may buy the child an expensive gift, like a cell phone and tell them not to tell anyone. Not long after this, the sexual contact starts.

If we can find a way to help people recognize these signs, we might be successful in keeping some children from falling victim to these abusers. It was in that moment that I realized that what happened to me could be used to help those people who have been abused, but more importantly, it could be used to help prevent a child from being abused.

I continued to surf the net and rack my brains until my vision got blurry. I realized that I had been online for over six hours. Suddenly I got exhausted, and was ready to shut it down for the night. I heard Stormy enter the room and I knew she was ready to go out. I apologized for making her wait and I took her out front so she could do her business and we could both go to sleep.

As I was lying in my bed waiting for sleep to come, I thought it would be a great idea to do a presentation at my church during child abuse month. My church had events for testicular cancer, breast cancer, and diabetes, but what about child abuse. I made a mental note to get on the net tomorrow and find out what month is child abuse month. Then I would contact someone at the church to see if I would be allowed to do a presentation.

The next day I called my pastoral minister to tell her about my abuse and how my life had changed, but I did not tell her it was because of *Book Number Five.* Then I told her about my idea to tell my story to the church during child abuse month. I wanted to get the drama ministry to help me re-enact some of the main events in my life so that we could shed some light on this growing epidemic and hopefully start some dialogue on how we can help those that have been abused, and most importantly, prevent the abuse from happening in the first place.

She liked the idea and gave me the number to the drama ministry. She also said she would talk to the pastor to get his permission to do the program, but encouraged me to go ahead and get started as if we already had the go ahead. I hung up and immediately dialed the number she gave me. I talked to the leader of the drama ministry and we set up an appointment to meet at the church the following evening. I arrived at the church around 6:30 p.m. the next day and sat in the pews waiting for Mrs. Beecher to arrive. As I sat there I remembered a time, not too long ago, when I sat right here one afternoon praying. The night before I had had dreams about mutilating myself and I woke up scared and feeling down. I spent that whole morning crying. I had never had dreams like this before and the vivid images of me using knives to gauge out my eyes stayed in my mind, refusing to go.

To help ward off these images and my suicidal thoughts I went to church to pray. I was the only one there. It was cool, quiet, and dimly lit. The only sounds I could hear were the sounds of the phone ringing and the sounds of the typewriter coming from the church office. I sat there crying unsure of what to say. How do you ask God to take you without it sounding like suicide? The last thing I wanted to do was offend a God that was already angry with me.

In between my sobs I would say how sorry I was for whatever it is that I had done to bring His wrath on me. I asked over and over again, "What have I done Lord to cause this kind of pain in my life? What do I need to do to fix this? I can't take much more. I just want to come home. Please just let me come home!" I cried for another twenty minutes or so before I could get myself together enough to go home. While driving home I came to the conclusion that this was a battle I wasn't meant to win and I just needed to go ahead and surrender.

My visit to the past was interrupted by Mrs. Beecher's voice, asking if I was Stephanie. I told her yes. We exchanged pleasantries and I began to tell her about my idea for Child Abuse Prevention Month. She jotted down a few notes about my story and we set a date to meet at the main church in two days. During that time she would pick the cast and begin writing the script for the program.

I drove home excited about the project and as soon as I got home I logged onto AOL, and sent an email to Susan outlining my plan for the drama ministry. I explained how I would tell my story during Child Abuse

Prevention Month. Susan responded to my email the next day. We hadn't seen each other since my insurance changed, just an occasional phone call and some emails. She wanted to meet as soon as possible to talk about my project. We set a date to have lunch at her office later that week.

Three days later, I was at her office for the first time since my company stopped using the insurance plan that allowed me to be in therapy with Susan. When I arrived at her office, I brought two things with me, I brought my lunch, and I brought the charcoal drawing of the peacock that I had done to give to her. When she saw it, she was shocked at how good it was and hung it on the back of her door so both she and her patients could look at it

We caught up on what was happening in both of our lives, and then she asked me to tell her more about my project with the church. I gave her a brief run down on what I was planning on doing and she asked me if I felt I was ready for that. I told her that I was. She thought it was a great idea and asked me to please keep her up to date about the project, and to let her know the date and time that I would be doing it.

For the rest of our lunch we talked about *Book Number Five*, Chakras, crystals and Shaman. When I left, I realized how much I missed therapy. Our meeting helped me to see that I needed to get back into therapy as soon as possible. I made a promise with myself that I would make an appointment with the pastoral care person at my church once I am done with the presentation at my church.

Two day after lunch with Susan I was at the church. Mrs. Beecher had selected two ladies and one man to help us with this project. She handed me the script and we began rehearsing. Halfway through the script, the man who was going to be the voice of Martin, stopped me in the middle of my speech, which would end the program. He walked up to me and put his arm around me and said this is a good script but it sounds like Mrs. Beecher and it needs to sound like you, after all this is your story. I agreed and began to tell each of the women my state of mind during the parts of my life that they would be portraying.

We wrapped up rehearsal and agreed to meet one last time on the Saturday before we do the presentation, which would hopefully be in two weeks. As we were packing up, Mrs. Beecher asked me if I wanted music. I told her I would love to end with the song *STAND*, by Donnie McClurkin. Mr. Johnson thought that was a great idea because Donnie McClurkin had been molested as a child and this is what he is singing about in that song. That was the first time I had heard that story and I immediately understood why that song touched me so deeply.

Mrs. Beecher liked the idea also and informed me that the band was practicing down the hall. I was hesitant at first. I loved that song so much and would rather play the CD rather than have the band attempt to play it. But I followed Mrs. Beecher down the hall anyway. I could hear someone playing the piano. We opened the door and stepped inside and there was a member of the choir talking to the guy playing the piano.

Mrs. Beecher approached both of them and then turned to signal me to follow. The man standing next to the piano player was tall and very handsome. I recognized him from the praise team and I knew he had a beautiful voice. She introduced me to both men and she began telling them about the program we planned to do in two weeks. She explained that we were just waiting for the pastor to okay the presentation because of the subject matter.

When she finished explaining everything, he gave me a great big hug. He told me that this was a great thing that I was doing and wanted to know how he could help. I told him I wanted to end the presentation with the song *STAND*, by Donnie McClurkin. The man sitting at the piano immediately started to play the song. He sounded just like the CD. The handsome man began to sing.

After the first verse I knew that the program was going to be great. The music was perfect. While he finished up the song, the minister of Pastoral care walked in and told us that the pastor approved the presentation. The only thing left to do was to re- write the script and help the ladies re-enact my life as best they could. I went straight home to work on the script for our final rehearsal. I was excited and scared at the same time. This will be the first time many of my friends will hear my story.

We met one last time the Saturday before the presentation. I went over the changes and we rehearsed the script that I wrote. When it came time for my summation, everyone agreed that it was perfect and reflected my personality. We hugged and ended our rehearsal and agreed to meet early Sunday morning so that we could do a sound check, go over positioning and say a prayer before we did our skit.

Sunday morning I went over my part once more. It wasn't hard for me to remember what I was supposed to say. After all, this wasn't a skit to me, it was a part of my life. After all of the preliminary preparations it was time for us to do our thing. The pastor informed the congregation that the drama ministry and one of the church members had an important presentation on child abuse that they wished to share.

We all took our places on the stage and we began. By the time we finished there wasn't a dry eye in the house. In fact the skit evoked so much emotion that the pastor forgot to take up the morning service collection. We were scheduled to do the same skit for the second service, but Mrs. Beecher informed me that there had been a change. My heart dropped because I thought she was going to tell me that the church members didn't want me to do the skit again. Instead, she said they are going to move our skit to just before the sermon, that way the pastor could do a special alter call for those who have been abused or know someone that has been abused.

Most of my family and friends came for the second service which started at eleven. When I invited people I didn't tell them what the service was about but I did encourage them to bring their children. My sister knew the subject of my skit but she didn't tell my brother or my mom who were both in town. After the skit I walked back to my seat to find the two rows of family and friends in tears. My sister gave me a great big hug and said, "Look what you did!"

I looked over to where she was pointing. There were over 20 people heading toward the altar to receive the special prayer by the pastor. There were a lot of people in the pews whose lives had been touched in some way by sexual abuse. I was both happy and relieved; I finally got the chance to tell what Martin did to me, forever removing the curtain of shame and the shield of secrecy that imprisoned me and allowed him to hide. It was the first time I told my story in public. My mother, sister, and brother were there as well as good friends and co-workers.

This was huge for me- to get in front of family and friends and complete strangers and tell the very thing I vowed to never tell anyone. What I believed would kill me, actually helped save me. When I left the church, I felt like I was worth something for the first time since I was nine.

For the rest of the month I had a table in the vestibule of the church with handouts and literature about child abuse. I handed out coloring books to children and ribbons to their parents and talked to both men and women about their experiences as children. Child Abuse Month was a success and I had taken another giant step toward healing. I was beginning to understand that by telling my story, I could help others who have gone through the same thing.

When I went to bed that night, I laid there happy about how the day turned out. I was evaluating my life and thinking about how one event can change who you become and how you see yourself in a world that allows an environment to exist where something as horrible as sexual abuse can occur. I realized that no matter how scared I am, eventually I will have to tell the whole story, every detail, because I know that someone out their thinks that some effect of sexual abuse is only happening to them and they need to know that they are not alone.

# 9

### *I LOVE WHO I AM*

*From the moment I was born people have been hating me.*
*No matter where I go there is always someone there*
*stereotyping me.*
*I live in a society that puts me in a category box and they*
*call it shaping me, while all along they are secretly bent*
*on destroying me.*
*I grew up on a block where a neighbor was always baiting*
*me, I was too young and innocent to realize he planned*
*on raping me.*
*I spent 43 years of my life hating me, constantly gaining*
*weight so there would be no dating me,*
*you see I couldn't trust anyone else touching me.*
*But, if you think life has me down, well your mistaken me,*
*because I am not weak but I am standing here powerful*
*and strong and there is no stopping me. I now know that*
*everything that happened to me went into creating me. If*
*I keep dropping knowledge like this, one day you will be*
*seeking me. I am powerful, beautiful and bold and there*
*is no changing me.*
*I love who I am!*

When I first wrote this poem, I really believed I was over what happened to me as a child. Although it definitely applies to me today, it wasn't truly accurate when I applied it to the way I was feeling and living when I wrote it. It was more like how I wished I felt. For me the effects of the sexual abuse were something that was very difficult for me to shake. My emotional health was fragile and easily affected by day-to-day encounters with people around me.

In the verse where I wrote "*No matter where I go there is always someone there stereotyping me. I live in a society that puts me in a box and they call it shaping me,*" was referring to how people would automatically make assumptions about who and what I was based on how I looked on the outside, never taking the time to explore who I was on the inside. She doesn't wear make-up, and she rarely wears dresses, and I have never seen her date or talk about a man in her life so she must be gay.

Basically, because I don't look or act like what our society believes I should, then there is something wrong with me. It was very hard growing up in a world where everywhere you turned you are told something is wrong with you and you don't fit in. Whether it was on TV, or in songs, during conversations over lunch, or with family, I have always felt like I was on the outside looking in. I am constantly evaluated based on stereotypes of how women should look and act.

As women we are always fighting for equality, yet we tend to treat each other exactly the same way most men do. I dared to not only step outside of the box of the common definition of how a woman should act and look, but I also chose to remain outside that box, even though it was extremely painful at times, especially when people said very hurtful things. I still didn't change I always remained the same, whether people understood me or not.

I wish I could say that I stood my ground because I was this brave young lady who was going to try to change the way women are viewed or to champion for those who dared to be different, but that would be a lie. I stood my ground simply because I didn't know how to stop being me. The truth was that I didn't wear make-up because my mom and sister rarely wore make-up. I didn't like dresses because the man who molested me often made me wear night gowns. Every time I put on a dress I was reminded of the abuse and I would feel vulnerable.

Finally, I didn't date because I couldn't chance being hurt. I believed that I was damaged goods and no one would want to be with me. The older I got the worse it seemed to get. The conversations and innuendos didn't change. Trying to explain why I didn't date, why I never had kids, why I prefer pants over dresses and why I never got married became more difficult because now, in addition to the guilt and shame, I was embarrassed about what people would think.

To explain these things would require me to share my story of betrayal, hurt, and depression and I just wasn't ready for people to know that part of me. I simply continued to ignore the chatter and the rumors. I learned to allow people to believe what they wanted to believe, regardless of if it was true or not. I'd rather have them believe the rumors, than to know the truth- I was afraid of life and all of the experiences that came with growing up.

Transparency with people, for me, was a recipe for pain. I didn't trust people around me with the truth because I believed they would use it as a weapon to harm me. I just couldn't take the chance of any more pain being inflicted on me. I knew I wouldn't survive it. I continued to live a lie rather than tell the truth. Even though the charade gave me the illusion of safety, it was actually a dangerous place for me to live.

It wouldn't be until fifteen years later that I would learn that the truth would make me free. Until that time arrived, I continued to act like I was happy go lucky, always smiling and making people laugh, trying to fit in with people who I knew weren't my friends because I believed I couldn't do any better. I allowed people to talk about me, drag my name through the mud, and question my integrity and character, and I never defended myself. Why? Because on some level, I believed that I deserved it. I put on my mask every day and played my role to perfection. No one knew the pain and despair that I was hiding, but I couldn't hide from me.

I played different roles. I would act happy when I was sad. Sometimes I would act sad when I was happy. I would act one way at work, another way at home and still another way when I was with family and friends. I had become so accustomed to changing the faces that I wore that I got lost and began questioning the real me. I didn't believe that the real "me" was good, or beautiful enough, or smart enough to show to the world, so I chose to hide.

But, the mask I was wearing obscured my vision; I couldn't see everything around me because of it. The mask I wore was used to hide me from myself and from the world. As long as I wore the mask, this warped view is the only view I had. So I lived with this view that only allowed me to see the darkness and never the light, which added to my despair. But I continued to wear it, thinking it would keep me safe.

The stress of trying to live my life for other people and the pain of believing that I was not good enough being me, was killing me slowly. I believe that God has sent each of us here with special gifts that we are supposed to share with the world, but somewhere along the way I started to believe that I wasn't worthy enough to shine. I was too afraid to stand out, to be unique and special so I settled for hiding behind those who I believed were smarter, more beautiful and more successful than me.

What I didn't realize at the time is that by denying my true self, I denied those around me the opportunity to experience God through me. I didn't get to experience the special and unique gifts God had given me. Although at the time I believed that I was walking on a path to a greater understanding of how the world works and how I fit within it, deep down inside I still believed that somehow someone made a mistake and I wasn't worthy to be on this journey.

Because of my inability to see and validate my strength, beauty and gifts, I saw the world through the eyes of self-doubt. My lack of faith in myself and in God kept me from reaching my goals. I always sought the lowest level in jobs and in projects. I was too afraid to stand out in any situation where my strengths would shine. Instead I hid myself when I should have revealed myself. I missed out on many opportunities because I didn't believe that I was meant for anything good.

So this is why I said, at the beginning of this chapter that I didn't fit what the poem said about me. I wrote this poem when I first was introduced to New Age Religion. For me it felt right, it felt good, and it made sense, but I was still empty. Even though I began to shine, according to those around me who were practicing new age too, looking back I can see that there were too many setbacks and relapses into depression. It was like a beautiful cake that lacked taste. I knew something was missing but I couldn't quite put my finger on it.

I didn't know it then, but the New Age Religion that I thought saved me was just a temporary fix that was so weak that my ugly past and depressed states leaked through occasionally, sending me right back to where I started. I wasn't drinking anymore, but I would still find myself depressed with suicidal thoughts, and would have to re-read *Book Number 5* to get myself back on track.

The book quoted the Bible often, but because I didn't know the Word for myself, I didn't know that the interpretations were skewed. Before I knew it I was hooked and pushing this book and the new age theology to anyone who would listen. I debated with Christians about God and their view and the Bible. I was convinced that I had found the truth, but I couldn't have been further from it.

I should have known that a book about God that never mentions Jesus or the Holy Spirit was not talking about the God of the Holy Bible. I was already sold on the whole, "I am god theme." I bought into their claim that there was no such thing as sin and that everyone is going to Heaven. I fell victim to this false theology because I didn't know the Word for myself. I allowed the people who were teaching me this New Age philosophy to interpret the Word and to tell me their truth about God. Even though I believed them, it still didn't fill the void that was there. The void was like a vacuum sucking the life out of me. I felt like an empty shell, and I desperately needed to be full.

In 2001, my sister and I brought my mother to Georgia to stay. She was diagnosed with advanced Alzheimer's disease and we were taking care of her. With this new situation, my friendships with the New Agers slowly dissolved and I was once again on my own. It was really difficult to watch my mother deteriorate right in front of me. She was such a dynamic business woman, poet and public speaker, and now she didn't even remember that I was her daughter.

During this time, I began online dating. At this time I had lost close to seventy-pounds and was starting to get some confidence. I talked to my sister about it and she thought it was a good idea. She had many co-workers who had met people online. I set up my profile on a site that was for plus sized people and I started to get hits. It was hard dating and trying to spread my wings while taking care of mom full time. We decided to move her down the street with my sister, and I helped her take care of her.

In March 2010, she died in her sleep at my sister's house, right before lunch. Her death and the death of my brother a few years earlier had left a hole in our family. We were all close, and now it was just my sister and I left. Growing up, I never thought about any of us dying. I couldn't envision a time in my life that I wouldn't be able to pick up a phone and call either one of them or go to visit. I could have used my mom's help and guidance with the issues I was struggling with.

I mourned the death of my brother, but I also mourned the loss of the information that he might have had. There was so much he could have told me about Martin and his family. Some of the information might have lifted the

141

clouds from my memories and helped me put those jumbled memories in chronological order. Maybe they could have helped me remember what happened that day in Martin's house in that upstairs bedroom.

Someone told me that if I put a picture of my brother under my pillow and meditate on it I could talk to him in a dream. I tried it, and on the third night, I had a dream about my brother. We were at his funeral, but he was standing in front of the casket, talking into the microphone.

He was teary eyed as he spoke, and he looked over at me often, and so did the other people at the funeral. They nodded in agreement to what he said, and at times shook their heads in sorrow. Everyone at the funeral could hear him, except me.

I remember talking to my sister about Susan wanting to meet with me to take me back so we could find out what happened, but she didn't think it was a good idea. She believed that maybe it is best that I don't find out. On one hand, I agree with her, but on the other hand, if I could remember what happened, it might give me the key to what happened to me. Sometimes when I am lying in bed, in the middle of the night, I get a sense that what Martin did to me, was also a set up for something unimaginable. Because of that missing piece of the puzzle, I don't have any hope of solving that mystery.

Although I didn't try *The Program* again, I continued to research it and try to find out if anyone else had the same experience that I had. It took some time before I figured out the correct wording to put into Google to find other people who had the same experience I did. One day while I was reading testimonies about people who did *The Program,* I realized that nothing was even close to what I had experienced. I knew I wasn't crazy and I know that it happened.

I was just about to give up when I typed in, "*I got trapped in a flashback while doing The Program.*" And the screen lit up. There were several people who said they got stuck in a flashback while doing *The Program* and some were trapped for almost a week, with no memories of how they got to families houses or to hospitals. Now that I knew I wasn't crazy, I needed to find out how this happened to me.

I looked up several theories concerning how we process memories and all of a sudden it came to me and this is my theory on what happened. During therapy, Susan didn't know that I was highly susceptible to hypnosis-something I found out in high school when I was hypnotized for weight loss. During one of the sessions, they had a hard time bringing me out of it, and although I could hear everything going on around me, I couldn't move.

In addition neither Susan nor I knew, until after the last time we did *The Program*, that I had a dissociative disorder. So when Susan started tapping and I started to concentrate on a traumatic memory, it threw me into a flashback. My mind didn't know that this event wasn't real, so I dissociated. This allowed me to stand outside myself and witness the little me experience the traumatic event.

I never met with Susan again and I never tried *THE PROGRAM* again. Looking back it was a good thing that I didn't. I don't think I was prepared to face what happened that day, and because of the way I reacted to *The Program*, something harmful could have occurred to my mind and it might have been the one thing, that could have broken me completely. I had to accept the fact that I might never know what happened. Eventually I stopped trying to find out and I accepted that maybe I don't need to know.

After my mother's death, I dove into writing and performing poetry at events. I also started writing my book again, and yes, I was still practicing New Age Theology. I had begun to try astral projection, moving things with my mind. I began consulting psychics, hoping to find the answers that would help me pinpoint what it is I need in my life. My journey to becoming whole was continuing and the next stop had the answers that I sought.

How did I miss this? It was right here under my nose all the time. The answer to the emptiness and a life that lacked meaning was here all along. I was just looking in all the wrong places, blaming the wrong people, and in reality not only was I hiding from the world, I was also avoiding the truth. You know what is the crazy part of all this? While I was seeking the truth, the Truth was actively seeking me.

# *10*

### *THE TRUTH*

*If you want to hear my voice, listen for me in the wind and in the rustle of the trees, that is where I speak. If you want to experience me, become aware of the beat of your heart, because with each beat you are made new. If you seek me don't look for me in the darkness, instead look for me in the light, for it will blind you to the world, and allow you to see heaven. If you want to see my face, simply look into a mirror and gaze upon the truth. In the truth is where you will find Me and where you will find yourself.*

As I continued to practice the New Age Theology, I met more and more people who were trying to figure out their life and their religious beliefs and I was always there ready to talk about my view of God and the universe, and the roles we play in God's production. One day I started to talk to a co-worker who was earnestly seeking the truth. He told me about a video, made by a minister that was really interesting. Not wanting anything to do with organized religion; I told him I would look for the video online, even though I knew I wasn't interested.

The next time I saw him he asked me if I had seen the video yet. I told him no, so he whipped out a DVD from his bag and told me he made a copy for me. He told me that he really wanted me to watch it because this minister talks about astral-projection, aliens, and other dimensions, and he wanted to know my thoughts about it. Well now he had my attention! A minister that talks about those subjects was a minister I wanted to listen to.

When I got home the next morning, I took the DVD out of my bag. For a quick second I contemplated watching it before I went to bed. I thought better of it and instead, showered, ate breakfast and slept for a couple of hours. When I woke up, I made lunch, fed and walked my dog and then settled in to watch the video. The first twenty to thirty minutes was about the Bible, and although I wanted to fast forward through that section, the minister insisted that people watching this need to get this background information in order to understand the rest of the video.

So I watched the biblical part, which turned out to be very informative and interesting. Then he got into the meat of his talk. The information that he presented contradicted everything that I learned and was practicing. The video, that was only two hours long, took me close to six hours to complete because I looked up every single thing he said. I looked up the Bible references, science references and any other information that he mentioned, and I was able to verify everything he said.

He floored me when he started talking about demons and people talking to spirits because we believe they are members of our family that have passed on. Some people are consulting psychics, and some are trying to astral project out of their bodies. But unlike ministers I have heard in the past, he actually explained why we shouldn't be doing these things. He told the audience that when members of our family die, they don't come back. That is not your family you are talking to, but demons that look like your family member so they can deceive you.

I sat up at this point because he really got my attention. He went on to say that when you go to a psychic, which I had been doing since high school, you don't know who they are talking too. I stopped the video there and thought of all the psychic parties we had at our house, and all the psychics we had gone to see over the years, but one psychic really stood out in my memories and I got really concerned about what my family and I had been doing all these years.

My mother had psychic parties at our house occasionally. She would cook up a bunch of food and make a desert and invite over twenty-five or so people. My mom would have a psychic, that someone said was really good, come over and she would sit in my mother's room and do private readings for twenty-five dollars. Half way through this one party, my mom pulled me aside and said she didn't think this woman was any good because everyone is going home after their reading and not staying around like they usually do to talk and compare readings.

My mother decided that I would go next. I was in my junior year of high school and had been to enough psychics to know if she was good or not. When it was my turn, I went in my mom's room and settled in a chair across from her. We greeted each other and she began the reading.

There are different types of physics; we usually deal with mediums, clairvoyants, or tarot card readers. This lady was a medium. A medium tunes into the spirit energy surrounding a person. Mediums rely on the presence of non-physical energy outside of themselves to receive information.

I placed my hands on the TV tray. She asked my name. I told her my name and then she asked me how long I had been having these awful headaches. I didn't know what to say. It took me a while to recover. I told her for about two years. The reason I was thrown off by her question is because I had a migraine headache all day. She shook her head and said, "I don't know how you take it my head is killing me."

At this point, she was already exceptional in my opinion. We continued on with her just flooring me with each thing she told me. It was as if she was inside my head and knew everything I was doing. It was crazy! She stopped the reading and was looking over my left shoulder, then she said, "Who is the person standing behind you with the initials MS?" I told her I didn't know, and she continued on with the reading telling me about my school work and about friends that I needed to be careful of. Then she asked me again about MS.

She went on to say, "He won't leave you alone. You knew him when you were kids" Again, I told her I didn't know anyone with those initials. She stopped for a moment and stared over my shoulder again. Then she added, "He was a boy you knew growing up. He drowned." I froze for a second because I knew exactly whom she was talking about. Michael Sparks, my first crush that had drowned at a pool party when I was fourteen.

After the reading, I found my mother and I told her that the reason people are leaving is because she is so good that it is scary. After my mom heard that, she pushed everyone back so that she could go next. After she completed all of the readings, she joined us at the dining room table and ate. She talked to us and shared her many talents that included mind control and moving objects with her mind. We sat around hanging on her every word. We had come across some pretty amazing psychics, but she was in a whole different category.

When I finally finished the video, I sat on my bed contemplating what I had been doing over these last ten years and my blood ran cold. I remember saying out loud, "Oh my God, what have I been doing?" I sat there for about twenty minutes thinking what I should do next. I called my good friend Tracy, who I introduced to New Age Religion.

I asked if I could come by even though it was late. I told her I had something very important to show her.

She said sure and then I asked her if she had anything to drink. She told me that she had some soda and juice. I told her I would stop at the store to get something for us to drink. By the way she said I will see you in a few, I could tell she was puzzled when I said that. Forty-five minutes later I was at the gate of her apartment complex waiting for her to buzz me in. When I got to her apartment, I put the bag I was carrying on the table. She asked me what I bought. When I pulled out a two liter bottle of coke and a bottle of 151 rum, her eyes got really big and she began to cry.

She asked me what was going on because she knew that I had not had a drink in ten years. "I just watched a video that has turned my whole life upside down, and you need to see it too." We poured our drinks, she popped in the DVD and we began to watch. Periodically she would pause the video and try to find some way of convincing herself and me that maybe what we were watching wasn't true, but she couldn't dispute the truth either.

This minister was successful in teaching us why going to psychics, astral projection and trying to move things with your mind was dangerous. He was able to explain, in a clear and concise way what the Bible said about these kinds of activities. He was able to expose the lies that we were told. During those two hours, he undid, what took us ten years to learn. We were at a loss for words because we realized that we were not on the right path.

After we finished, watching the DVD, she looked at me and said the same thing I did, "What have we been doing?" All of a sudden, all those catch phrases like "I am awake, and my third eye is open", and "I have a broader understanding of God than the sheep", now sounds so ridiculous. Turns out we didn't know the first thing about God because we let other people tell us who God IS, rather than take the time to sit down and read the word for ourselves.

We both believe that Jesus knew we thought we were on the path to God, so He came back for us. We spent the next couple of hours talking about how crazy we were for doing what we were doing, and how we thought hearing things and seeing dark figures was proof that we were open. The only problem was, at the time, we didn't understand what we had been opening ourselves up to.

On the way home I was scared, relieved, and lost at the same time. I was scared because the rug that I had been standing on for my sanity for the last ten years was snatched from beneath me. I was relieved because I now know what I was doing wrong and will stop it immediately. I felt lost because I had no idea what I was supposed to do next. It was like I had moved to another country and was excited about the trip, but when I got there, I realized I didn't have a clue about the culture or the language.

When I got home, the first thing I did, was get on my knees and apologize to God for what I had been doing and I begged for His forgiveness. Although I wanted to do some more research, I was too exhausted so I went to bed. For the first time in ten years, I slept with the light on because I was more than unnerved. The supernatural events that I had been experiencing validated everything he said. I couldn't run from the truth, because the truth was already in front of me.

I found more of his videos and after watching a few I became interested in reading the Bible. Now I expected people to be shocked, but what I didn't expect was how many people expressed their disapproval and concern about me reading the Bible. People told me that the Bible was written by too many people and couldn't be accurate; another told me that it was fiction. But instead of discouraging me, they made me want to read the Bible even more.

I was suspicious that the Bible must have some truth to it, because so many people were trying to get me not to read it. No one ever tried to discourage me from going to the male strip clubs or watching porn, or drinking, but me reading the Bible was cause for concern. So I began reading the Bible, and before I knew it, I was hooked. This was the most accurate history book that I had ever read, and it was prophetic as well. When I read Matthew and saw how Jesus handled those Pharisees and Sadducees who tried to cause people to doubt him, I was amazed.

Jesus became my focus! I found a prayer online that had me confess all of my sins and declare that Jesus was my Lord and Savior, and that I believed He was born of a virgin, died on the cross for our sins, and rose after three days. I repeated that prayer three times to make sure that God knew I was serious. I didn't know that when you turn your life over to God all hell breaks loose.

I began having crazy things happen to me. They were happening so frequently, that Tracy called her cousin, who is deliverance minister. After she told him of the supernatural events that were occurring, he told her that he needed to see me. Tracy called me and said we need to take a trip.

My cousin said he needs to see you. So the next time we were off, we packed up her car, and Tracy and I took a four-hour road trip to see him.

When we got there, we ate lunch and were just relaxing in the living room when we heard a knock on the door. It was her cousin Sebastian. He came in and gave me a hug and we sat down and began to talk. He started off by telling me that he has known my calling since I spoke at their family reunion a while back. He was just waiting for me to realize it. Then he asked me about what was going on. I told him about the sleep paralysis, and other events, but I also told him that I didn't think it had anything to do with the sexual abuse.

He said it had everything to do with sexual abuse. The devil can't create anything new so he uses what he knows scares you. "You have to understand that the devil is mad that he lost someone like you, because he knows your gift of speech and how people listen to you. He is going to do everything he can to scare you away from God, so I need you to get some confidence because you are going to be battling."

I so wished I could have laughed that day, called him crazy and went back home, but I knew he was right because of what was happening in my house. We finished up talking and before we headed to his church, he told me to keep an open Bible in my room, either on the bed, the night stand or under the bed and call on the name of Jesus with confidence and faith. He hugged me again and left for church.

At the end of his sermon he called me up to the front of the church. I was surprised, but I got up and went and stood by him. He prayed over me and said that he would be my covering. He prayed a prayer of protection over me and asked God to cover me in the Blood of Jesus as I stepped into my calling. I thanked him for his prayers and for talking to me. As we drove back to the house, I wondered what calling he was talking about.

On the way back to Atlanta Tracy and I talked about all of the things that had happened to us over the last few years. We both were very happy that we had truly found our way and we said we would start doing Bible study in the upcoming week. The rest of the way home, we went back and forth about me setting up a camera in my room to see if this stuff was really happening. Tracy thought it was a bad idea. What was I going to do if I see something? Plus I already know that it is real.

Over the next few weeks, we dove into the Bible. We started with Matthew and we loved it. We went from talking about crystals and *Book Number Five*, to talking about the Lord and how wonderful He was and thanking Him for saving us. During this time, I didn't realize that I was changing. I am not talking about not watching porn anymore, or no longer attempting to astral project. I am talking about changing how I thought, watching what I said, ridding my house of anything new age, both trinkets and books and seeing God in everything.

Just as Sebastian predicted, I battled nightly. Calling on the name of Jesus was my weapon and my battle cry. I noticed that instead of being afraid of what was happening; I had a sense of peace that had come over me. That confidence that Sebastian said I needed, was growing each time I stopped an event by calling on that Name. One morning I woke up and I realized that this was for real. Don't get me wrong, I believe in God, but when you really try to grasp the concept that God is real and the Bible is true your mind struggles with it.

I now know why it is so hard for us to understand the supernatural, it's because we live in a natural world. Because of this, I now accept that I won't understand everything. So, I just keep reading, believing and trusting in God, knowing that He will reveal things to me when I am ready. And that is exactly what God did. A few weeks later

He gave me a revelation that could have only come from Him and this was the pivotal event, that started me on the path to a whole new life.

I woke up, one Monday afternoon, after finishing an extremely busy three-day weekend at work. I was too tired to get out of bed so I pulled my laptop over to me and logged on to Facebook. I noticed that I had a friend request but decided to save it until I finished looking at my news feed. After about an hour, I felt like I was ready to get up and get lunch. I clicked on the friend request to see if it was somebody that I knew.

I didn't recognize the name, but there was something about his face that seemed familiar. I checked to see if we had any mutual friends, which is the first thing I look for before accepting a friend request from people I don't know. We didn't have any mutual friends. I returned to the picture. I couldn't see it clearly so I copied and pasted it in into an app so that I could make it bigger. I couldn't believe who it was.

When the picture became larger, I instantly recognized that face; it was Martin, the man that sexually abused me for years, except he was using a different first name. He was still short, had that wispy mustache, and he still wore gold-rimmed glasses. I sat there staring at the picture for about ten minutes, trying to figure out what would make this man contact me. I thought about what Susan had told me about him wanting to maintain contact, but what Sebastian said made more sense. The devils will bring something from your past that he thinks will scare you.

Then I realized something. I wasn't scared, I wasn't angry, and I wasn't sad, in fact I didn't feel anything. Now if this had happened just a year ago, it would have destroyed me. I would have either killed myself or would have found him and killed him. Many times, over the years, I tried to find him by putting his name in Google and using the key word pedophile or child molester. I just needed to know if he had other victims besides me. Now, I no longer need to know anything about him.

I deleted the picture and I denied the friend request. When I did, it was the first time I had ever seen Facebook reply to a denial with the message, "This person will not be able to ever contact you again." "Since when did they start this," I said to myself. I closed my laptop, put it on the bed next to me and then I did something that even shocked me. I got on my knees and I prayed for Martin. Then I prayed for the victims whose lives were forever changed by him. I thanked God, because I knew that I was healed from what Martin had done to me.

Later that day I met with my friend Tracy and I told her what happened on Facebook. She jumped up and said, "When are we riding out to go and get this dude?" I laughed and told her we are not going to do that because I have given this man too many years of my life already and I refuse to give him anymore. She asked me what he wanted. I told her I didn't know, and it didn't matter. Whatever it is, it is between him and God at this point. I had forgiven him and I am no longer haunted by him; that door has been shut and sealed.

The next day I had lunch with my sister and told her the story of Martin sending me a friend request on Facebook. She had the same response as Tracy, and I told her the same thing I told Tracy. I refuse to give him any more years of my life. She was shocked when I told her that I prayed for him right after I deleted his profile and picture. How did he find you on Facebook? I told her that I think he searched for me because we didn't have any mutual friends on Facebook. Then I told her what my thoughts were, about him trying to contact me signified.

I told her about the story of Job and how Satan went to God and challenged Job's faith and trust in God. God told Satan that all that Job has was now in his hands but do not kill him. I went on to tell her that I imagined Satan going to God and telling Him, "I am about to mess your girl up!" And God replying, "Go ahead and throw that card, because she belongs to me now!" This sums up how I feel about this situation.

God was letting me know that because He healed me completely that Satan could no longer use that to scare me. As we sat there finishing up lunch, I could feel that I had closed a major chapter of my life and was about to start a new one. I wasn't sure what it was, but I could feel the stirrings of something great in my spirit. I started spending more time with God and the more time I spent with Him, the more I changed. I made a conscious effort to stop cursing. I stopped watching television and listening to secular music because of the language and the lustful thoughts they caused. I just concentrated on reading the Word.

*Book Number Five* didn't come close to the kind of joy I was feeling now. Unlike the feelings that New Age gave me, there were no undercurrents of sorrow. The cloud of depression was completely gone, and I truly loved life. I knew that this was permanent, and what amazed me the most about all of this, is I don't remember praying to God to take it away. It came with me turning my life over to Him.

For the first time in my life I didn't feel fragmented. I began to see how all of the pieces of my life were coming together to make a glorious picture. Most importantly I was able to see how even the pieces that caused the darkest times of my life fit the puzzle perfectly. Without those pieces, the picture wouldn't be complete. God was showing me that everything is in perfect order, even though they felt like they were out of place. They fit right in where they were supposed to fit. They all are responsible for creating who I am today.

# 11

## *I LET MY SOUL RUN FREE!*

*Oh what a wonderful year this has been for me, you see, I dared to let my soul run free.*

*I stretched out my arms with my face toward the sun, and as a result a new life I begun. Twelve months of peace and joy from within, for the first time in my life, I feel comfortable in this skin. There are no words that exist, that can describe how I feel, so that's why I give thanks each time that I kneel.*

*All of my past problems have been washed away, swept out to sea and it's a brand new day.*

*I never thought that this day would come, but I wasn't surprised where my peace came from.*

*You see, I finally trusted in God and He did deliver me, He blew away my storm clouds and calmed my stormy seas.*

*So now I want to tell my story of how I made it through, and I want to the whole world to know that the same can happen to you.*

*All it takes is lots of faith and an understanding of who*
*you are, and then God can come in and lift you up and*
*make you his shining star.*
*So the next time, when your world turns black, and you*
*can no longer see,*
*Open your heart, trust in God and let your soul run free!*

After the Graduation, my housemate and I had lunch to celebrate her graduation. We then headed back to the dorm. I went to my room and put on some gospel music and began listening to one of my favorite songs, *How I Got Over* by Mahalia Jackson.

*Tell me how we got over Lord*
*I've been falling and rising all these years*
*but you know my soul look back and wonder*
*how did I make it over!*

As I sang along, the tears were streaming down my face, but for once, these were not tears of sorrow, but tears of joy and triumph because I know how I got over.

During the past year, I have lain awake in my bed and looked back over my life and I can see how God was with me every step of the way, even in that dark basement. I am sure that His heart broke that I had to go through that, but He knew that when I came out on the other side of this journey I would be made new. He knew that I would be well prepared for the next stage of my life.

God confirmed this to me while I was reading the Bible. He pointed me to the scripture 1Peter 5:10. God let me know that I needed to go through what I went through, and because I endured, I am rewarded with Peace and Joy that fills every part of my being.

*"And after you have suffered a little while, the God of all grace, who has called you to his eternal glory in Christ, will himself restore, confirm, strengthen, and establish you."*

He has done what He promised. God has restored me. Restore means to return someone or something to a former condition, place or position. I now have that joy and love of life that I had before those tragic events of my childhood. I no longer pray for death. Instead, I pray for the deliverance of others who find themselves in a dark and lonely place where they believe that God has forgotten them or has left them there to suffer alone.

God has confirmed me. To be confirmed means that a person is firmly established in a particular habit, way of life or belief and is unlikely to change. After completing my forty-two-year journey and coming to a place of joy and peace, I know that God never left me. He was always by my side. Although He pushed me to the limits of what I thought I could take, He knew that I could take it. All of this has solidified my love, trust and faith in God.

God has strengthened me! When someone is strengthened, it means to make or become stronger. This is definitely true for me. As a result of the things that I have had to face, I have become stronger and wiser. I understand that there is nothing that I cannot overcome as long as I have God in my life. When situations come up, I settle myself by saying, "This is nothing compared to what I have been through. I have been through far worse." I stand in the storm, and instead of seeking shelter from the rain, I now welcome it.

God has established me! To be established by God means that He was able to make me strong, complete, and equipped to follow Him and to face the trials that exist in this life. All of my little battles have prepared me for the bigger battles that have yet to come. Now when I am faced with adversity, I am no longer at a loss for what to do. I give it to God, and I remember how I got through all those other battles. Those battles have provided me with skills that will help me survive whatever situation comes my way.

People have questioned me about my belief in a God that would allow me to go through such pain. I tell them that the God I serve has not asked me to experience anything that He hasn't. Jesus was lied on. His name was dragged through the mud. His integrity was questioned. He was falsely accused of a crime He didn't commit. He was perfect, yet they found fault in Him. As a result, He died a horrific death on the cross so that we could be saved.

I remember the day that I came to an understanding of why I went through all of this. I believe I found the answer in John 9:1-3 As *he went along; he saw a man blind from birth. ² His disciples asked him, "Rabbi, who sinned, this man or his parents, that he was born blind?" "Neither this man nor his parents sinned," said Jesus, "but this happened so that the works of God might be displayed in him.*

When I read this scripture, it all became very clear to me. For all of those years I thought God was punishing me for something, but in actuality, He had chosen me for something- so that He could show His works. When God shows what He is capable of, it can't be anything small; it has to be something big enough so that those who witness it will say, "Look at what God has done in her life!"

Then I asked myself, knowing what I now know about God showing His works, in the future when dark days come my way, will I approach them differently? Will I cry out to God asking Him why me or will I drop to my knees and thank God for choosing me. I know that He is going to use this situation for the good of someone or something. Will I be able to maintain my faith when it looks like I am in an impossible position and there doesn't seem to be a way out? The answer is yes! I have already been there and God came through in a miraculous way.

Because of what I have been through, and how I came through it, people that I meet who have gone through the same thing or something similar, will be able to see how happy and at peace I am. Perhaps that will give them that glimmer of hope to hold on and to not give up. If I had been successful the day I had planned on killing myself, I would have denied someone the gift that God sent me here to give him or her.

I believe each and every one of us has something important to give this world, but we fall prey to situations, and get ensnared in the traps of the enemy. We forget that God sees and knows all. He has already made plans and put people in positions to not just free you from that situation or trap, but to also heal you and elevate you to the next step. Failure is not an option in God's Kingdom. We are children of God so failure should never be an option for us either.

What all this has taught me about God is that He is a God of patience and timing. I was quick to think that God was saying no to my prayers. I believed that God wouldn't answer them at all. I believed that He had simply forgotten me when in reality He was waiting for just the right time to deliver me. I have since learned to trust that God is actively working out my situation and when the timing is right He will answer my prayers.

Right now I am working on being obedient to God, even if what He tells me to do doesn't make sense to me or simply sounds crazy. I do it because I trust Him. I am still enrolled in school so that I can learn everything I can about the Bible. I want to be able to discuss it and defend it intelligently and bring people to God. Most importantly, I am trying to spend as much time as I can with God so that I can develop a sound relationship with Him.

How has all of this changed my life? Besides the obvious peace, love and joy that emanates from me, I have totally turned my life over to God so that it will be His Will done and not mine. I trust God with everything I have, and the only thing I have is my life. I have surrendered it to Him in totality. When I consider all that I have been through, I can honestly say if it took for me to experience all of that pain and suffering to get me to where I am today, then it was all worth it. Even if I could, I wouldn't change a thing.

I have been trying to write this book for over fifteen years. It didn't take that long because I didn't know how to write, it was because I started over at least ten times. Each time it ended up saved to my hard drive until the next time I decided to start writing again. At least two of the four had really good stories, but there was always something that didn't sit well with me, so I would stop until I got the urge to try it again.

Fifteen years later I met a life coach who I told that I had at least seven books in my head. He told me, "If you come see me, I will pull them out." A few months later, I called him, and for the next year minus four months somewhere in the middle, we met monthly. At each meeting he would ask me what I planned to have completed by the time we met again. At the next meeting he would pull out the list and would go down it to make sure I had completed everything.

During the time that we spent working on this book, I re-wrote it at least three times. The first two times he understood, but on that third time he wanted to know what was going on. I told him that I wanted to write a novel and hide my story within it, but God wouldn't let me write it that way. I didn't want to write an autobiography because that is a lot of really personal information to put out there.

He simply told me that I had to get out of the way because this book, my book, is going to help a lot of people.

Needless to say, this has not been an easy book for me to write, because it required me to go back to the darkest and scariest times of my life. In order to write it in such a way that the reader can really understand the impact that those events had on me, I had to get back into the mindset that I had during that time without getting lost in my past. I thank God that He accompanied, directed and guided me during the entire process of writing this book. That is what helped me to work my way through it until it was complete.

I have poured my heart and soul into this book. I have been way more transparent than I had planned to be, but God wouldn't have it any other way. I now understand the reasons and the importance of the transparency. Someone who has gone through anything like this will find comfort in knowing that they are not the only one that has experienced some of the after effects of sexual abuse. That will hopefully encourage them to seek help so that they can begin the healing process.

`I trust that God will use me and this book in ways that will help others heal. If that means that I might have to sacrifice some of the things I want, like a husband and my dream home, then I am willing to make that sacrifice for Him. I know that the rewards that await me in heaven will far out weight anything that the world could ever give me. God has put me through the ringer and I have survived it. As a result, He has raised up a spiritual warrior.

My prayer for this book comes from Isaiah 55:10 *"For as the rain and the snow come down from heaven and do not return there but water the earth, making it bring forth and sprout, giving seed to the sower and bread to the eater, so shall my word be that goes out from my mouth; it shall not return to me empty, but it shall accomplish that which I purpose and shall succeed in the thing for which I sent it."*

Just as God's Word goes out and doesn't return void, I pray that this book will be like the Word of God. I pray that it will go out and not return void, but accomplish that which God purposed, and succeed in the thing for which God sent it.

In Jesus' Name I pray Amen!

From this point on I will be doing whatever God needs me to do, whether it's writing books, teaching in the classroom, or preaching in a church, I will be obedient. I will do everything I am supposed to do. When I reach the end of the road, I don't want to look back and wonder how

I got over. Instead I want to look forward to joining God, who brought me over. On that day, I want to be able to stand before Him knowing that I have exhausted every gift that He has given me and I can tell Him, "Lord I am ready, and I have no regrets."

# NO REGRETS!

*When my time here is up and I go to meet my maker, I want to be able to stand before Him and say, that while I was here, I did the best I could, to love myself, and everyone else around me. I want to be able to tell him that all my dreams were realized and all my goals were met. I want to be able to say to Him,*

*Lord I am ready, and I have no regrets!*

*I want to be able to tell Him that it was during my darkness hours that I saw the light, during my weakness moments that I found strength, when I was fearful, that's when I found courage, when I felt foolish is when I found wisdom, and it wasn't until I was lost, that I found my way. I have paid my dues, and I have paid my debts,*

*Lord I am ready, and I have no regrets!*

*I want to look back over my life and re-experience all the ups and downs, with the understanding that in certain situations, I might not have made the best decision, but at the time it was the best that I could do. My time here is up, and there is no more time to fret.*

*Lord I am ready, and I have no regrets!*

# I LET MY SOUL RUN FREE